The Sh̶̶̶ elias

First published May 2006 by Shalom House Poetry, 31, The Cairn, Newtownabbey, County Antrim, BT36 6YF.

ISBN : 0-9551896-3-2
       978-0-9551896-3-0

©Copyright for the poems and short stories remains with Noreen Campbell and Denis O'Sullivan.
No part of this book may be reproduced or transmitted in any form or by any means without written permission from the publisher, except by a reviewer who wishes to quote brief passages in connection with a review written for insertion in a newspaper, magazine or broadcast. All information contained within the book is correct at the time of going to press.

Printed by Summit Printing
137 Gregg Street, Lisburn BT27 5AW
Tel: 028 9266 5038   Fax: 028 9266 1471
Email: info@summitprinting.co.uk

The cover is a reproduction of a painting 'Sand Dunes, Rosbeg' by Comhghall Casey, 1998.

This book has been funded through the support of the 'Awards for All' scheme.

The Shore Fields

Noreen Campbell
&
Denis O'Sullivan

Acknowledgments

The Shalom House Poetry Group gratefully acknowledges the Awards for All scheme for its generous funding and support of this publication.

Thanks are due also to the Belfast Institute of Further and Higher Education (BIFHE) and the Shalom House Centre, Cliftonville Road, Belfast.

Particular thanks to the members of the Shalom House Poetry Group who helped edit and proofread the material.

Some of the poems included here have been published previously in ***The Lonely Poets' Guide to Belfast (2003)***, ***Ringing the Changes (2004)*** and ***BT1 The Poet's Code (2005)***, all published by The New Belfast Community Arts Initiative. Both authors also contributed to the Shalom House Poetry Group anthology, ***Keeping the Colours New***, published in 2003.

The story "Colours" first appeared in the ***Black Mountain Review***, issue 12 Autumn/Winter 2005/6 and "Not at this Address" in ***Ireland's Own***, March 2006.

The story "James", in an abridged form, was one of the first to be read on the Radio Ulster ***My Story*** series in 2004 and was included in the Radio Ulster ***My Story*** book published by Blackstaff Press in 2006.

The story "Talking to Pickles" was first published in ***Abracadabra 3*** (2000) by BIFHE.

"Hijack" is based on an incident related to the author by Brendan Henry.

For Caragh and Lawrence

For Mary

After retiring from nursing, Noreen Campbell turned to creative writing, drawing on her experiences from a rich and varied life for her prose and poetry.
Born in Inch Island, Co. Donegal, she grew up with the hardships of rural life in the thirties and forties. The beauty of her birthplace, a small island surrounded by Lough Swilly, is deeply woven into Noreen's writing. She is a member of the Shalom House Poetry and Creative Writing Classes.

Denis O'Sullivan was born in Belfast but spent his childhood and early teen years in the Co. Antrim village of Glenavy and, despite having lived in Belfast for most of his life since then, he retains a close affinity with his rural upbringing.
Educated at St. Mary's Christian Brothers' Grammar School and Queen's University, Belfast, he graduated as an electrical engineer in the early sixties, but soon transferred into the rapidly developing field of computers.
In recent years his lifelong interest in writing has been rekindled by the Shalom House Poetry and Creative Writing Classes.

Incoming tide — poems by Noreen Campbell

Inch Island	11
Grandfather	12
Granny	13
Evening visit to a graveyard	14
Insomnia	15
Unwelcome	16
Reminder	17
The Shore Fields	18
Visiting Annie	19
Nature	20
Farewell to Marceline	21
Belief	22
Who needs it?	23
Coming / Going	24
Incoming tide	25

James and other stories — Noreen Campbell

The evening robin	29
Sour milk	33
James	39
An awakening	43
A friendly matter	47
Straw for thought	51
John and Dan	55
Talking to Pickles	57

Getting there — poems by Denis O'Sullivan

Funfair	63
Sugared almonds	64
Heron	66
Looking at an old photograph	67
Rebirth	68
Flying a kite	69
Ploughing	70
Walking by	71
Finger in the brain	72

The journeyman reaper	73
Partners	74
Japanese painting	75
Another world	76
Getting there	77

## Colours and other stories	Denis O'Sullivan

Mary's house	81
Colours	87
Mother's attic	91
Hijack	93
Not at this address	97
After the funeral	103
The money tree	105

Incoming tide

Noreen Campbell

Inch Island

The hills are taller now,
or am I smaller now?
For many years have come and gone,
many moons have shone upon the waters of the Swilly,
since I first left you,
dear Inch Island.

The fields were greener then,
or was I keener then?
For many years have come and gone,
many moons have shone upon the waters of the Swilly,
since I first left you,
dear Inch Island.

Some day I will return,
and rest among my own.
And many years will come and go,
many moons will show their light upon the waters of the Swilly.
No more I'll leave you,
dear Inch Island.

Grandfather

Stepping the long field
he'd move steadily forwards,
head tilted against the weather,
his mind calculating
as to the measure of land,
type of soil,
suitable for potatoes
or a year out for grazing?
Always the right decision was made.

A legacy of care
handed down with the land.

Granny

Your memory sublime
as I recall your stories of
once upon a time.

The voice silent
as I stand beside your chair,
a time just lent.

Sun and sand,
dresses of silk, ribbons for hair,
you made our Disneyland.

Good memories shine
ever new, sewn in my love
for you.

Evening visit to a graveyard

Evening falls, and soon the moon will rise to chart its silver wake
while I, my heart in shreds, dread the thought
that I will perish one day,
and wonder who will cherish my memory?
Then tears fall and I hear the distant call of a bird,
and from its sweetness
I ask the Lord to hear my prayer:
If to dust I must return
wrap me in birdsong.

Insomnia

Breaking the quiet of the night
a dog barks.
From behind a parked car, a cat runs for its life.
Stars dance in a blue sky to their own noiseless sound,
bare trees stand sentry-like
while the moon casts their shadows
ghostly across the ground.

Standing at my bedroom window,
sleepless in Belfast,
the scene unfolds.

Unwelcome

There's a cracking sound in the night,
Death! The noise calls.
I hear the beat of running feet,
the thud as a body falls.

And here, where once a family lived,
are people, soulless with grief,
mourning the person who loved them.
No voice, no touch, out of reach.

Yet still our flags fly from lampposts,
Glory, their message clear.
Shame, I shout to the running feet,
you are not welcome here!

Reminder

I stand on Baylett shore:
the brown hills of Burt
rise up towards Grianan;
the grey stone of Inch Bank
separates fresh and salt waters;
the purple sunset over Errigal Mountain
lights the distant sky.
All these memories of childhood
enshrined in the colours of a silk scarf.

The Shore Fields

At an oíche mór he'd sing, loud and clear.
His voice would bring great delight to those gathered,
"Sweet as a nut," they'd mutter,
others said,
"Clear as well water,"
and many a mother hoped he's fancy her daughter.

The old folks cried when he died young.
And now of a summer evening,
when shadows grow long,
he can be heard singing in the shore fields,
a lonesome song.
"Sweet as a nut," they mutter,
some say,
"Clear as well water,"
all say,
"Go ndéana Dia trócaire air."

Visiting Annie

I'm baking bread, she said,
nodding her head towards the oven-pot hanging on the crook,
its lid glowing with red hot embers.

I'm baking for them, she said,
nodding her head towards a framed picture hanging on the wall,
its image blurring with time and soot.

It's good to bake, she laughed,
prodding the chaff towards the old dog lying on the hearth,
its body pulsating from heat and sleep.

Do you want a piece, she said,
nodding her head towards the slices of bread on my knee,
their crusts dripping with butter and jam?

It's good to be alive, she said,
nodding her head towards the clock standing in the corner,
so I went home to Mammy.

Nature

Burgeoning begonias, whites, pinks and reds,
tumble from terracotta pots.
An explosion of colour, they spill on Carrara marble,
defiant of its purity.
The message clear in their ruthless vigour:
No storyteller in paint greater than Me.

Farewell to Marceline

Your long Winter is over.
Bud forth in the Spring of Heaven.
Flower sweetly in your eternal Summer.

Belief

Some day soon
I'll stand on the high hill
gaze across the lough
and see the blue waters merge with the mountains.

Some day soon
I'll plough the lea field
gaze along the furrows
and feel the brown earth weigh down my feet.

Some day soon
I'll dance with you once more
gaze into your eyes
and know the love we shared will never fade.

Who needs it?

Sunny weather brings housework in abundance,
curtains to be taken down
washed, ironed
and, worst of all,
hung up again.
Balancing on a pair of steps
blinded by material
groping for rings
head buzzing
then the realisation,
wrong curtains on wrong windows.
Now it starts all over again,
balancing
groping
unhooking
as swear words and prayers mix.
The phone rings,
should I answer?

Coming / Going

I come from an island,
a beautiful place
where Swilly waters drape the shore
like a silver thread.

I come from a National school,
all of two classrooms
where a free standing blackboard
resembled a coal boat.

I come from a hospital,
a different world
where the care of the patient
bound us together.

I come from motherhood,
a joyous time
where the needs of children
outweighed future plans.

I come to grannyhood
an exotic island
where a new generation
greets me with joy.

Incoming tide

Quietly I walk the shore,
wet sand yielding to my steps,
cold wind biting my face,
while the tide tumbles inwards.

Loudly the grey gulls' cries,
echo across the froth frilled water,
small boats riding the swell,
while the tide tumbles inwards.

Lonely in the winter twilight,
black rocks, displaying wreaths of wrack,
white stones pearling on the beach,
while the tide tumbles inwards.

Happily I walk the shore,
pleasant memories flowing all around me,
sweet childhood returning to delight,
while the tide tumbles inwards.

James
&
other stories

Noreen Campbell

The evening robin

Emily Dunne cut a small figure as she stood between the brothers John and Pat Bodel in their garage on Mount Road.

"Will you not let me drive you home?" John asked.

"No thank you," she replied, "the older I get the more exercise I need; the joints are getting stiffer, John. Cars are the ruination of us all."

"Don't say that or you'll wreck our business," John laughed. "See you at eleven tomorrow."

"Good night, gentlemen," said Emily and walked smartly from the forecourt.

"Emily's one of life's ladies. That's a pleasant surprise she got today," Pat remarked.

"She's all lady," answered John, making his way over to rewind the air hose.

It was only a ten minute walk from Bodel's Garage to Emily's home, The Lyons House. Night was closing the tired eyes of day and hoar frost clung on the grass verge and briar-clad ditch. She marvelled at the patterns made by the minute icicles on blade and branch, when a robin, flying deep into the frosted briar, startled her.

"You're a noisy little fellow," she said aloud. "Maybe I frightened you first. Anyway you should be nested by now."

She walked on, aware that the fright had triggered her old headache. She thought of the robin and remembered her mom's saying, *An evening robin seeks a soul for Heaven,* to which her Dad would reply, "Rubbish, Mary Lyons."

She pushed open the gate and walked up the avenue to the front door. Snowdrops, untroubled by frost, grew in clumps on the lawn. Martha had left the hall light on as usual.

Martha was her dear and trusted daily, who, like her mother before her, took care of the Lyons House and its occupants. She cajoled or threatened Emily as situations demanded.

"New curtains would brighten up this room," she would tell Emily, and if Emily agreed, she would add cushions to match, knowing where they could be bought and at what price. If Emily disagreed Martha would say,

"My mother would turn in her grave if I left those old rags on the windows, I'd never be able to face her in Heaven."

And so Martha would win the day but always to the benefit

of Emily. Martha was indeed a rare treasure.

Opening the door Emily stepped into the hall. Aware that the heat inside was quickly defrosting her face she wiped her eyes and nose. Throwing her gloves on the table she saw the telegram and, touching it, she said,

"It's true, it's true."

Her eyes fell on the note propped against the brass backed clothes brush and she read,

Back at eight to cook for tomorrow – Martha.

Going into the sitting room Emily poured a sherry and overshot the glass. She mopped the spillage and sat down, her dull headache persisting. She spread her hands on her lap and surveyed their landscape. Tremor? No, no visible movement, small strong hands, small like Mom's, strong like Dad's.

Mom and Dad, she thought, Mary and Peter Lyons. They had met as medical students, fell in love and got married and, she, Emily, was the result of that love. She was an only child but never a lonely one. Though busy doctors, her parents afforded her much of their time and an abundance of their love. Emily looked longingly at their photograph on the mantelpiece and whispered,

"Michael is coming home tomorrow."

Michael Newel was the youngest in a family of four who lived in The Heritage, the house that neighboured on theirs. With brothers Jack and Tom, and sister Lisbet, he went to school with Emily. How vivid now in her mind were the games they played together, Tom and Lisbet on one side, Michael and she on the other. Jack always managed to be on the winning side.

"He cheated," she thought, "and got away with it too."

How they laughed through those happy, happy days of childhood and occasionally wept when a much loved pet died.

How quickly the time passed, school, college, university. She and Jack decided on medicine and it was in this very room they hugged and cried before parting.

"You would think you were going to America," Dad said.

"Or Africa," said Michael, and they all laughed through their tears.

Emily's mind took her to another parting some years later. This time they stood in an airport lounge, and with breaking hearts, said goodbye to Michael, bound for the African Mission fields.

It was that same day she first met Bob Dunne. Blinded by her tears she walked straight into him as she made her way from the lounge.

"Sorry," she cried, "Michael's gone."

"Your boyfriend?" he asked.

"No, indeed not," she replied, "Michael is just Michael."

"Well, that makes everything crystal clear," Bob said. "Let's have a coffee."

Soon, she found herself telling her life story to this complete stranger.

Though her head ached, Emily revelled in her reverie. She recalled her wedding day; the look in Bob's eyes as her Dad put her hand in his; Michael's telegram saying "I love you both"; a year later the birth of their son, Patrick Robert, like herself an only child; the next twelve years with all their happiness.

And then the burning memories came. She shivered.

She could still hear the voices, feel the comforting arms, but the anguish on Jack's face at the hospital realised her worst nightmare.

"They hit black ice," were his only words.

She cringed like a wounded animal, the pain of her loss unbearable. Michael wrote faithfully to her, each letter recalling the details she had written to him about Bob and Patrick. Oh God, how the very sight of their names tore at her heart. And then, sometime in the last fourteen years, Emily found herself writing to Michael telling him all the things she could remember about Bob and Patrick.

Fourteen years since they had died, she thought, and Michael is coming home tomorrow.

Emily heard Martha open the door and she snapped back to reality. Her thoughts turned to tea and she rose quickly.

Martha heard her fall and was soon by her side.

Later that week John and Pat Bodel walked the snow-covered road to church. They slipped quietly into the seat beside Martha who was in her own silent world of grief. Michael was already on the altar, the vestments hanging loosely on his thin shoulders. The smell of incense filled the church as his emotion-filled voice intoned,

"Receive her soul and bear it to God Most High."

And Pat Bodel wept for one of life's ladies.

Sour milk

Wee Johnnie Rocks stirred sleepily in his bed. He pummelled his cheeks and eyes with warm chubby knuckles, rubbing sleep away, trying to waken up. Birds were singing shrilly outside the bedroom window – the dawn chorus. His Daddy had told him about it, how one bird sang out early in the morning and wakened all the other birds who joined in the singing. His Daddy said they were thanking God for their beautiful singing voices, but when he told this bit of news to Paddy Burke at school, he just laughed and said,
"Your da's a wally."

Johnnie went over to the window and looked out. It was a lovely bright morning, the sun already well risen, the blue sky threaded here and there with wispy white clouds. Then he heard that same noise again, the noise that had first disturbed his sleep. He smiled, knowing it was his Daddy getting ready for work.

He had such a great job, Johnnie thought, pushing his feet into his trainers. Just imagine driving a bus all day, super duper. He hurried down to the kitchen and was greeted by,
"How's Johnnie this morning? Tea?"

Johnnie nodded and was soon sitting behind a mug of tea, toast and the top of his Daddy's boiled egg. They chatted about football and agreed that Derry would tear strips off Tyrone on Sunday.

"It's only half six son, why don't you go back to bed for a while?"

"Can I go into Mammy's bed?"

"No. Let your Mammy sleep a bit longer. Take a book or a toy with you. See you this evening."

As Johnnie went back up the stairs his happiness faded somewhat. Last night came vividly to mind, and Sean O'Dwyer and his death. Sean was just another wee boy in Johnnie's class in school. He used to get sick in class and fall on the floor and shake. Master Johnston was very good to him; he never shouted, just turned him over on his side and wiped his mouth. Then he would put him to sit in the Master's chair. The only other person allowed to sit in that chair was Father McBride, the school inspector, who had beady eyes and a sharp tongue, unlike Sean who looked dazed and sleepy. When Johnnie said this to Paddy Burke, he said,
"Sean looks stupid because he is stupid."

Johnnie told his Mammy what Paddy had said and she was very cross and said,

"Don't ever repeat anything that comes out of that boy's mouth."

Johnnie climbed back into bed still thinking of Sean. He sat hunched, leaning his chin on his drawn up knees, going over what had happened that day. He could see it so clearly, running out of the school gate, Paddy Burke dragging his schoolbag behind him, Sean in front with Pat Lynch, and the others horsing around. They had just turned into Bishop Street when it happened. Sean stumbled forward and fell. He didn't shake, he had a grin on his face and Paddy Burke said,

"Get up you eejit," but Sean just lay there.

A police Land Rover came down Bishop Street and stopped. Trevor Black and the other police jumped out. Trevor knelt beside Sean and put his ear close to his face, then he said,

"Ambulance! Quick!"

Sammy Lynn used his walkie-talkie saying,

"No, it doesn't look good."

Rob Bryce told the boys to go on home and Johnnie heard him telling Paddy Burke to clear off. Johnnie knew all the police because the barracks was in his street.

When his Daddy came home in the evening he sat down and took Johnnie on his knee. He talked about what happened coming from school.

"Sean was a very sick boy," Daddy said, "and God took him up to heaven."

Johnnie cried and then came the excitement of the funeral. The school was closed for the day, and the boys had to stand outside the church.

"Stand up straight, hands by your sides," Master Johnston told them, and they did as he said. Johnnie whispered to Paddy Burke that Sean died because he was very sick, but Paddy replied,

"He did not; the fucking police killed him."

"Sean's in Heaven," his Daddy told him, "just forget what Paddy Burke said." And he had, until last night, when Granny came.

Johnnie was in bed but Granny was so noisy and loud he got up and listened at the top of the stairs.

"You're well oiled tonight again, it's great you can afford it," said Daddy.

"I'll not drink much of yours," she shouted back.

"I've nothing for you to drink," Daddy said, "I've nothing to spare when I keep my wife and son."

"Your son?" she screamed, "he's not your son, Jimmy Boyle, and you're married what? Five years? And you've produced nothing! Some use you are."

Daddy didn't answer but Johnnie could hear Mammy scolding Granny. Granny kept quiet for a while then she said,

"What did you think about Sean O'Dwyer? Some carry on that was. They say if Master Johnston had been there, they say it was the police's fault, they say they'll sort out the police. They'll get even and good for them, I say."

"Listen Granny," Daddy shouted, "don't bring your rotten politics into this house. I don't want to know what they say! I don't want to hear that kind of talk in this house again. You've less sense than Paddy Burke."

"Kiss my arse, Jimmy Boyle. No wonder you're crying, love, married to yon thing. You're only an excuse for a man," she spat at Daddy, and flounced from the house.

Mammy asked Daddy for a glass of milk and then Johnnie heard her being sick in the sink.

"Don't fret about your Mam," Daddy said, "she had a drop too much."

"It's not that," said Mammy.

"Is the milk sour?" Daddy asked.

"No! It's not that either," said Mammy.

After that Johnnie didn't know what they were talking about because Daddy was saying,

"YOU'RE NOT!" and Mammy was saying,

"I AM!" and Daddy was saying,

"WHEN?" and Mammy said something Johnnie didn't hear so he went back to bed and slept.

The clink of bottles brought Johnnie back to the present. It was Peter Green, the milkman. He'd go out to Peter and then he might even go to 8 o'clock Mass. If he went to Mass Father Bradley would ask him in for his breakfast, saying,

"When you're with me she can't nark."

There was nobody to nark him, there was only Rosy the housekeeper, and she was so nice. When she'd bring Father in his breakfast, she'd look at Johnnie and say,

"Oh, and are you here this morning again?"

Johnnie dressed in a hurry and came downstairs. His

Mammy called from the kitchen,

"Is that you, Johnnie? Where are you going?"

"I'm going to help Peter," he said.

"Don't make a nuisance of yourself," she said.

"No, I'll not. I might go to Mass," he said.

"Going for your breakfast more likely," laughed his Mammy.

Johnnie dandered up the street still thinking of last night, Granny shouting about the police and Sean, about him not being his Daddy's son, and Daddy saying Granny was oiled. A man came once and oiled Mammy's sewing machine and made a mess of it. Daddy said the man had used the wrong oil, it was far too heavy. Maybe that's what's wrong with Granny; he thought she must be using heavy oil. He liked his Granny so he would tell her to drink lighter oil.

Johnnie stopped at Hegarty's gate and waited for Peter. Peter was a tall man, eyes bright with the morning air and black, curly hair close cropped to the scalp.

"What about you?" he greeted Johnnie.

"Alright. How do you carry so many bottles in each hand?" Johnnie asked Peter.

"I drank lots of milk when I was small," Peter said, swinging up his arms and putting the empties into the crate.

"Here," said Peter handing a carton of orange juice to Johnnie, "drink that and you can help me do the other side of the street."

Johnnie sucked the sweet orange juice and decided his future. He would be a milkman in the mornings and a bus driver after dinner.

Peter turned the milk float, pulling tightly in against the high hoarding of the barracks.

"How's Peter?" Steven Crowe called from the sentry post.

"Grand," called Peter, "and yourself?"

"Should be off but Trevor's not in yet," said Steven.

"That fellow's always late," laughed Peter.

"Are you helping Peter?" asked Steven.

"No, I'm drinking orange," Johnnie replied.

Both men laughed and the conversation was over.

Peter gave Johnnie a bottle of milk and told him to leave it at number 63 while he left three at 61 and three more at 59. His next delivery was to Miss Hill. She was a nice lady with a nice house and a nice garden.

"Nearly finished," Peter called to him as he carefully closed the gate with the black plate and gold lettering which read, "V. HILL No. 57".

"That's that," said Peter, "do you want to come over to the White Wall while I eat my sandwiches or do you want to go to Mass?"

Peter knew all about Rosy and her aggro towards Father Bradley and how Father used Johnnie to get his own back on Rosy. Peter also knew that Rosy would be Rosy long after Father Bradley had gone.

"Well! What's it to be?" asked Peter.

"The White Wall," Johnnie answered.

The White Wall was at the top of Lomax Street separating it from a patch of waste ground, on which had once stood a thriving shirt factory. It was now the Parkhead dream of every footballer in the school. Peter lifted a bottle of milk and a carton of orange juice, and fishing out a large parcel from between the milk crates, he remarked,

"Keeps them nice and cool."

He waved to Steven, still on duty.

They crossed the street to the entry which joined Johnnie's street to Lomax Street. Peter strode on, keen to eat, while Johnnie stopped to pat Hegarty's dog. He was a big, black Labrador called Punch. Johnnie hugged Punch who licked him all over, especially the orange juice from his mouth. He followed after Peter and halfway through the entry he could see the White Wall. Peter was already there, and he saw him put the milk and juice on top of the wall. Then Peter took a step backwards, stretched out his arms, and gripped the top of the wall. Swaying slightly he spewed with great force.

"Go back!" he shouted to Johnnie. "Go back and get Steven. Tell them to come!" And again he puked violently.

Johnnie turned, ran through the entry and across the street. He called to Steven,

"Peter's sick, very sick, he's spewing down at the White Wall, and he said tell them to come."

A shiver ran through Steven as he pressed the bell and relayed the message to the desk sergeant. Then he dashed down to the White Wall.

Peter looked at him, ashen faced, blue eyes glancing with shock.

"Where's the pain, Peter?" Steven asked. But he got no answer.

Peter released his grip on the wall and pointed towards the waste ground. As Steven followed the direction, he moaned aloud,

"Oh Jesus no! Not Trevor!"

There was no doubt, not from there. Face down he lay, the blood soaking around his head like a halo.

The Land Rover rattled up Lomax Street and stopped. The sergeant and three policemen got out. This time Steven pointed over the wall. The sergeant looked and turning to him said,

"Would you stay on duty for a while longer?"

Steven turned and walked up the entry, meeting Johnnie coming down. He didn't speak to him and Johnnie thought this very odd. As he neared the wall Peter came to meet him. Wiping vomit from his blue overalls he took Johnnie's small hand in his.

"Were you sick, Peter?" Johnnie asked. "What made you puke?"

"Don't know." Peter said.

"Was the milk sour?" Johnnie asked.

"Very sour." Peter replied.

James

"No love, no friendship can cross the path of our destiny without leaving some mark on it forever." François Mauriac

And so it was with my first love. Did I know it was love? No, not then.

It all began one day during my summer holiday. I had, at sixteen, gone to visit my elderly friend Maggie. She told me incredible stories about local people, their hardships and survival. She told me about the deaths of her two daughters within twenty-four hours of each other. She taught me how to bake Boxty bread and how to pick and string bilberries on long grass strands. I ate as many as I strung but there were no cross words, just a mere chide,

"Don't stain your frock or your mother will be cross."

Her husband James was a very tall man, all of six foot four. He was a fisherman and was accordingly dressed in a gansey and glazed peaked cap. He was a man of few words, speaking only in answer to Maggie's questions.

"Did you flit the goat?" she'd ask.

"I flitted the goat," he'd reply.

Maggie and I had gone to pick bilberries and when we got back James said,

"She'll be late."

"Aye, she'll be late," Maggie said looking at the clock.

"Will you?" she asked.

"Aye." He replied, putting on his cap.

"Go with him," said Maggie and I followed the tall, silent man, taking five steps for every one of his.

We arrived on the shore stones and he unceremoniously lifted me and set me in the boat. Putting the oars in the rowlocks, he set out for the Mill Bay. This, I knew, would see me home safely for teatime. Rounding the Drum Point, he asked,

"Would you like to pull an oar?" and stretching out put the oar in my hand, all the while rowing steadily and placing my hand flat and firm on the oar.

"Now," he said, "Keep your oar straight and your eyes on my snout."

I did both and soon we reached Mill Bay. As I jumped out onto the sand James said,

"You've got the knack, you're a good listener so you'll be easy learned. Ask your father."

I skipped up the road and on Drumtinney Brae I looked back over the Swilly. He was about to pass the Skart Rock – a distance of three miles – but he saw me and raised an oar high in the air.

I asked my father and soon I was an avid and apt pupil of this elderly man. James taught me all he knew about rowing and six weeks later we won our first race at the local regatta.

After the race he gave me a bar of toffee, a bag of brandy balls and a two-shilling piece, saying,

"The toffee's for eating, the brandy balls are for Maggie and the florin's for keeping."

A few days later, I manned the oars while James baited codling lines. I watched the big spade-like hands put the worms on the hooks and drop them over the side. After the lines were dropped we idled, waiting for a bite. Suddenly he spoke,

"They were two lovely wee lasses, just your age when they died. We couldn't do anything just watch them go. It was sore on Maggie, aye, it was sore on everybody."

I had no answer for James. Instead I shipped the oars and taking my lunch bag I went up and sat beside him. I gave him one of my two squares of chocolate and he told me he had never tasted chocolate before. This big man talked of his heartbreak, the poverty of people, the kindness of neighbours and the cruelty of consumption. We got a fair catch and when he threw the bag of fish over his shoulder I slipped my hand into his and we walked home together. For the next two summers we rowed and we won races, but most of all we talked. He boasted openly that I was the best lass ever to put a hand on an oar. Maggie confided that he was more like himself now, and I brought him the occasional bar of chocolate.

When I told him I was going to Belfast to train as a nurse he said,

"Watch you don't catch some ould disease up there."

He gave me the bailing shell from the boat, a brown marly stone and a half-crown.

On my visits home, I brought him chocolate. The big frame was shrinking and there was a marked stoop to the once square shoulders. Rowing time was over for him. Then my mother wrote the dreadful news that James had cancer of the mouth. I made my way home complete with chocolate. But nothing prepared me for what I was about to see.

A skeleton of the man I knew sat at the fire holding a cloth to his mouth. The cancer had eaten through gum and lip and the saliva flowed steadily. When the cloth soaked it was thrown on the fire. His speech was affected but his eyes told me that he loved me. I sat with him and held the cloth to his running lip. When it was time to go I knew I would never see him again. Again I had no words for this man, all I could do was put my hand on his shoulder. He promptly covered my hand with his and mumbled, "keep your oar straight, lass, and I'll meet you in Heaven."

If hearts break, then mine broke that night for a man sixty years my senior, a man admirable in his skill and knowledge of boats and tides, a man of humility and great strength, a man who definitely left a mark on my life.

This was James, my first love.

An awakening

I watched the hands of the clock climb slowly to eight. I had slept fitfully and it was a relief to know I could get up without disturbing Rose. The air conditioning was noisy, but when I turned it off the heat was unbearable; how far away and how pleasant seemed the wet summer of home.

I was on holiday in Philadelphia, staying with my cousin Rose. I looked around the room taking in its opulence, from the inlaid mahogany furniture to the carefully positioned television. The colour scheme of mushroom pink and pale green was easy on the eye. Everything oozed old world charm, from the beaded covered carafe to the dainty dish of boiled sweets by the bedside. This was my sixth day here and I was living up the lavish lifestyle.

I went into the shower room and smiled as I saw the disposable slippers.

"Used slippers cause foot-rot," Rose had said, so I went with the flow. After showering I dressed in a terracotta and cream outfit but it only added to my already bulky appearance. So, I opted instead for a navy and white dress and went down to breakfast.

Rose, at eighty two, was in full flight with breakfast. I settled for juice, cantaloupe and a slice of pumpernickel. A retired dietician, Rose was a generous host and extremely rich.

"I'd give it all up to have Fred back again," she said.

Fred, her late husband, had been a forensic scientist with the police department. His passion had been cars and he had made no secret of his loathing for black people.

Dot and Hughie, my cousins, arrived with their daughter Barbara to take me to lunch in Atlantic City. We departed 8062 Rowland Avenue, North Philadelphia, in a silver Dodge Caravan with dark tinted windows. I felt like someone in a film as we headed south across Walt Whitman Bridge, which spans the Delaware River, and onto Route 95 South through New Jersey. An hour and a half later we were in Atlantic City. We went via the AC Expressway to the casinos where everything was bigger than big. We kicked off in The Show Boat on Delaware Avenue and the boardwalk, where Hughie gave me a roll of quarters saying,

"You lose that, you don't play no more."

Luck was with us so, at one thirty, we went to the Show Boat restaurant. If the restaurant was grand, the food was grander still.

From the eighth floor the view of the Atlantic Ocean was stunning.

After lunch we tried The Taj Mahal and again our luck held.

We came out onto the boardwalk, bathed in clear bright sunshine. Photos were being taken when I heard Dot gasp and Hughie say quietly,

"He's a vet."

"How do you know?" she asked.

"Gee woman, I know that tattoo."

I looked left and saw, hanging on two wooden crutches, the skeleton of a man, a placard hanging from his neck which read:

I'm dying from Aids. I'm homeless. Please help.

A small bucket sat at his feet. I stared in disbelief at the spectacle. As Dot went towards him Hughie took my arm and walked away. When Dot caught up she had tears in her eyes as she said,

"He's some mother's son."

I shopped as usual, getting tee shirts printed for my grandchildren. After that the offer of coffee was a welcome rest, but I was totally amazed at the plainness of the café. It was a strictly no frills affair and, after the grandeur of The Show Boat, quite an eye opener. Dot told me all the boardwalk cafés were the same.

"But just you wait," she said.

Hughie treated me to jelly sticks made from twisted pastry and jelly. Heaven never felt closer than then. Jelly sticks are totally addictive and gorgeous. We gathered our shopping and once more stepped into the bright sunlight.

As we were making our way back I felt Dot's arm tighten in mine. An ambulance, flanked by two police motorcycles, stood on the boardwalk. A crowd had already gathered. The emaciated body, slumped on the ground, was being checked for vital signs by a blue clad paramedic. The hushed silence was broken by someone asking,

"Anything I can do, officer?"

"That son of a bitch don't need no help now," came the terse reply.

As they closed the zip of the body bag I saw a young woman take the begging bucket and disappear into the crowd.

We drove home in silence. Later in my room I tried to reconcile my day with that of a dead stranger, his abject poverty, my magnificent lunch, his begging bucket, my traveller's' cheques, his body bag, the luxury of my room.

"Oh God," I said aloud and as Rose handed me a coffee she said,

"Dinner is booked for seven thirty at the Rose Briar; that's the other face of America."

I felt like vomiting but I dressed and went with the flow.

A friendly matter

I watched the pale hands of dawn push the lingering night from the sky. At last I found I could get up after a restless night, and if I wakened anyone, so what?

Coming into the kitchen I made the usual cup of coffee. It tasted bitter, bitter and empty like my life this morning. I sat in space for a long time, when footsteps on the stairs jolted me back to the present. I flew into the room and turned on the lights on the tree, as a voice inside my head beat out a message, "normality at all costs."

Margaret, at fourteen, asked,

"Did Santa come?"

"To you? At your age?"

She smiled when I told her there was a small present on the table, but that she knew the arrangements about the presents. By now other, older bodies appeared in the kitchen, Gerard, seventeen, Patricia, twenty one and Hugh, twenty two. Their gloomy mood was palpable. As I made pots of tea and coffee someone asked,

"Are we going to nine?"

I replied, "Nine."

We went to Mass and some folks wished us a happy Christmas, but most avoided us as it was easier for them. It was a relief to get back home. There were lots of phone calls, all well intentioned. Many people called, cushioning their discomfort at our situation with asides, such as, we were passing so we just dropped in, must call with so and so etc. By one o'clock I felt like screaming,

"Why the hell did any of you come? We don't need your pity," but instead, I nodded and assured them I understood their haste.

Patricia and I prepared the dinner, while Gerard and Margaret fought over setting the table. Hugh had slunk off with a book as usual. I was emotionally wrecked by now, and was glad to call out,

"Time to open the presents."

We tore into the opening as if we had never had a present before. All were bigger and better than usual; all of us had joined in an unplanned futile act of compensation. The ping of the oven called us and we trudged through piles of paper and sat down to dinner.

Silence reigned like an unseen guest as we picked at our festive fare. Suddenly Hugh pushed his plate across the table and shouted,

"It won't ever be the same!"

And I heard myself reply in an ice cold voice,

"No."

We left the dinner that never was, and with Margaret and Gerard in tow I began to clear the table. The rustle of paper caught my attention and I went in. Patricia was tidying up and was obviously crying. I told her to leave it as we would have no more visitors tonight. I returned to the kitchen to referee Gerard and Margaret as to who was doing more than whom. I dreaded the night to come and wondered if I could cope.

Hugh thudded down the stairs just as the doorbell rang. I heard the laughter long before the face appeared in the kitchen. Only one person could make such a noise, and yes, it was Uncle Seamus, followed closely by his wife, the ever gentle Auntie Maire. Maire was my friend from student days and since parenthood we had become honorary aunties and uncles to each other's children.

Uncle Seamus seemed to be a moving mass of noise, talking to everyone at once. He held Margaret firmly in a head lock, while tugging Hugh's height of fashion shirt and asking,

"What old alco did you swipe that from?"

Maire, still in the kitchen with me, said,

"He was such a good person."

I looked at her and saw her eyes brim with tears. We stood for a while in our private moment of grief and then went in to join the others. Uncle Seamus greeted us by asking,

"Did you hear the one about the man who hung up his sock with a big hole in it?"

I never heard the rest of the story as laughter was everywhere. He sang, Patricia played the violin, Margaret the guitar, and when I showed him the poetry book, *Around the Boree Log*, he recited from it *The Lad from Tangmalangmaloo*.

Maire and I made supper and everyone ate heartily making up for the earlier disaster. The craic went on long into the next morning. Around three o'clock Uncle Seamus decided it was time to go home, remarking how his cousin Frank would be rising to open the shop and if I needed any bacon he would run over and get it. We laughed and as they put on their coats, I quickly wrote in the poetry book, "For you, from us." I handed Seamus the book, and when he read the message, he looked at me, put his arm around Maire and walked away.

Dawn was clawing the night sky as I climbed the stairs. I had had a happy night thanks to true friends. I had heard their laughter, and had sensed their hidden pain at the loss of their friend, my husband. My first Christmas as a widow was over.

Twenty one years have passed since then. Maire is dead. *May her gentle soul rest with God.*

Uncle Seamus still visits, still makes me laugh and still sits to three in the morning.

Straw for thought

Paddy presses his big calloused hands against his forehead and silently wonders about his present situation, held in the barracks, and all for keeping the law. The Thatcher was right all along in his opinion of the guards; they're a bunch of culchies from Mayo, most of them pulled from the bogs there.

He shifts uneasily on the hard chair which is playing havoc with his thin backside and this discomfort is bringing to the fore an anger that he, Paddy Boylan, is not known for. He had hoped to see Guard Devlin tonight, a young fellow new to the barracks, whose father had worked for Paddy's father years ago but he didn't seem to be on duty.

Nothing is going right for Paddy.

Nothing had gone right since Sunday, when, under instruction from The Thatcher, he set out to find Chook's body. Chook was a young drifter who worked between The Thatcher and himself for five years or more until he left a month ago to work on the factory ship at the mouth of the lough. Three weeks later a notice in the local paper informed its readers of the untimely death of one Chook Boardman due to falling from The Night Light and consequently drowning. The body was never recovered.

Everyone was shocked and for the next nine days they waited in grief for a young man they had taken to their hearts. Then the search for the body began, but no trace of it was found. At two pm on Saturday The Thatcher appeared in Paddy's kitchen with a big roll of paper under his arm.

He was a coarse featured man, brief and direct in conversation.

"It's day ten", he said, "if the body's not up by now he's impaled on an anchor, lots of anchors down there, never lifted, once the big boats come in."

He unrolled the paper and Paddy gazed at what could only be described as a morass of lines.

"That," said The Thatcher, pointing with gnarled forefinger, "is the factory ship, these here the tides running fast and high, these here the floodgate waters, the moon is three quarters so the drift is to north east. If the body floated, he's up here in Slate Tongue."

"And what?" Paddy asked.

"The Guards are watching me, and I wouldn't please that sergeant to lead him to the body, so it's up to you, Paddy. Take Conemarra with you, she's a good dog and knows the shoreline well."

At half four on Sunday morning, Paddy left the shelter of Hannah's old wallstead and headed round the shore with Conemarra. Dawn was just about breaking and the silver grey of the eastern sky added an eeriness to the remainder of the night. He drew long and deep on his fag and patted the dog for both their comfort. Together they reached the Slate Rock and the climb was anything but easy. The dog negotiated the rock with the agility of a mountain goat, and Paddy was left to his human struggle. At last he topped the Slate Rock and heard the dog give a bark followed by a whimper.

"I've made it, girl," he called, and again the dog whimpered.

"Have you hurt a paw?" he asked, easing himself down onto the shale.

Paddy looked towards the dog and saw her nuzzle something up at high water mark. Stepping forward with all the nerve he could muster, he saw it was a body. He dropped to one knee and sure enough it was Chook. The crabs had not been kind to his face, but there was no doubt. It was Chook.

"You poor bugger," Paddy prayed and then screamed,

"Jaysus! No!" when he saw the two legs tightly bound by rope.

Conemarra came up and whimpered, moved away and whimpered again. Paddy edged towards her for company, his face grey as the shore, and his mind boggling out of control.

"Come on, girl," he said, "we'll head home and tell them."

The dog didn't move and whimpered loudly.

"Are you hurt, girl?" he asked looking down shore, only then seeing the other body. This too was a young man bound hand and foot. His stomach turned and he retched violently. Then he headed through a cutting in Slate Rock. This was no man's land, but deranged by shock, Paddy was fearless. He came out eventually in the Bog Meadow and ran all the way to The Thatcher's.

"You found him?"

And Paddy nodded his head as he drank the well laced strong tea while The Thatcher got on his ship to shore radio and called the coastguard.

"Aye, I'll take you in. No, I'll take my own boat, half an hour. No, Paddy Boylan."

The conversation ended there.

"We had better go up to the barracks and tell the culchies." But the guards were already coming up the lane, the coastguard having called them.

They were civil to Paddy who told it as it was, but The Thatcher lost it when the sergeant said he would go with him.

"Not in my fecking boat you won't," he spat at him, and when the sergeant said he could impound the boat, he went off totally.

"The Slate Tongue's not a bog hole in Mayo, thicko, and you can get yourselves up it." The veins in The Thatcher's neck swelled with blood and he wiped away the froth from his mouth as the sergeant quietly left.

Paddy's guts tightened as they neared Slate Tongue, but all was as he had seen it earlier and sadness and anger flowed freely. The Thatcher picked a horse whelk from Chook's arm and crushed it with vehemence. All were surprised when the sergeant took The Thatcher's arm and walked him back to the boat, and more surprised when The Thatcher didn't object. All went home to their own houses. No one spoke.

Paddy was out feeding the cattle when the sergeant and a guard arrived in the yard. It was exactly a quarter to five.

"We're taking you in for questioning; get your coat."

Paddy got his coat, and went with them.

Now it's half ten on Monday night and he has not been asked one question, just handed mugs of tea and plates of sandwiches. When he asks, no one knows anything.

He picks slate slivers from his hands and sucks the sores to clean them. The detention room door opens and Guard Devlin comes in. Paddy notices the two mugs on the battered tray. He doesn't even close the normally locked door behind him.

"You took your time. Thought you didn't want to know your friend, but then it was your father was our friend, not his son."

Guard Devlin laughs,

"Shut up, Paddy. I've news for you. Did you hear the racket earlier on? A big move's going down. They're going to impound the factory ship and arrest the captain and crew. It seems the Guards knew that something was going on. The Thatcher's been watching them and it's on what he told the sergeant they're going in. The Thatcher and the sergeant are going in first in the patrol boat. There's even a Garda diving team up from Galway."

"And what the hell have I got to do with it?" Paddy yells, his backside so sore now that all reasoning is gone.

"Oh, you're being kept in here for your own safety. It's a real gangster set-up, hard men, very dangerous. They think the two lads came across something, and look how they were treated."

"Poor unfortunate buggers," Paddy says with respect, "but that's little ease to my arse; it's cut in two on this friggin' chair."

"Why didn't you fold up that blanket and sit on it?"

Cut to the quick by this reminder of his own stupidity, Paddy retorts,

"What do you take me for? Some sort of a floozie?"

Both men laugh and Paddy asks what time they're expected home.

"Around six, sure we'll see the lights once they hit the Fort Road. I brought in some stuff to fry; I'll be doing it in an hour if that's alright. You can be mother!"

"I'll knock your block off me bucko." And both men laugh again.

Guard Devlin is annoyed that Paddy has been wrongly treated but he can do nothing to change that. He'd heard many stories from his father about the kindness of Paddy's father - "treated me like a son he did."

Paddy reads the young man's thoughts and says,

"The sergeant's the sergeant."

"Tell me, Paddy..?"

"Tell you what?"

"Why is he called The Thatcher?"

"Well," Paddy says slowly, "he doesn't drink, doesn't smoke, just chews straw."

"Serves me right for asking," Guard Devlin sighs.

"Where's the pan," says Paddy, "I'll fry."

John and Dan

The water ran freely into the cooler at the top of the Glen field, and John Bogue was very pleased with himself. He rattled an old bucket with his stick and the cows came lumbering up from the hollow. He shooed them over to the cooler, and a big grin spread across his big red face as he watched the grey tongues slosh the water.

It had been hard work getting the water this far, digging with a spade all the way down from the side of the hill, but such a bonus now to see the cows drinking. He lit his pipe and sat down on the ditch to survey the results of his labour and work out the best way to take the water into the Castle field and maybe the Bog meadow. He drew contentedly while he soaked up the heat of the sun. This is the life, he was thinking, when a voice cut across his thoughts. It was Dan Duffy, a man John hated with a vengeance.

"Aye, grand day," John responded to Dan's remark.
"You've plenty of water."
"I have."
"I was thinking I could take a branch for my cattle."
"Your cattle? - two ould scrawny bullocks."

John was fuming for Dan had refused to let him cut across one of his fields with the pipes, forcing him to go the long way down the hill, causing a lot of extra work and more expense. John could not believe that Dan was thick enough even to ask for a supply and thought, "not on your bloody life," but aloud he said,

"Naw, I don't think so."
"What do you naw think?"
"I don't think you're going to get any of my water."
"It's unlucky not to share water."

John noted the veiled threat in Dan's words and exploded.
"Bad cess to you Dan Duffy, don't you threaten me; you're nothing but a parasite, a selfish bugger; look at them two animals of yours, half starved they are. Get off my land or the only water you'll need will be to wash the blood off when I'm finished with you."

"Aye, well," Dan mumbled.
"Aye, well nothing, clear off."

John puffed his pipe and a bigger than usual smile spread across his redder than usual face, as Dan shuffled off, muttering,

"Tight arsed ould whore."

Talking to Pickles

Jane Dodds woke with a shiver.

Where was she?

She looked about with sleep-laden eyes and saw furtive forms dancing around the room. As wakefulness returned, she realised the forms portrayed the struggle between the gathering dusk and the firelight. Her gaze searched for, and found, the clock on the mantelpiece. It told her half four.

Something slid from her knee, and as it thudded onto the carpet, she remembered. She had come in and sat down to read a new recipe book that her daughter Mary had sent her, and she must have fallen asleep in the comfort of John's big chair.

"John!" she exclaimed. "It's nearly teatime and I haven't prepared anything."

She must hurry. But she could not move. Her legs were powerless, just a numbness, a void.

"Oh my God!" she cried. "I've had a stroke. I haven't been asleep. I've been unconscious. Oh no! John, John, where are you?"

John was her dear husband of forty one years. They had first met at university where she was doing biochemistry and he was a veterinary student. They were good friends as far as he was concerned, but as for her, Jane McCay, she adored him. They met at dances and other social gatherings, and always ended up in each other's company. Then came graduation and parting. Jane was sad leaving her class mates, but broken hearted over her friend John Dodds.

She remembered her Dad saying,

"You're not like a girl with a good degree under her belt."

She could picture him yet; big brown arms spread on the gate, as he pensively eyed and judged the ripening corn.

"I'll have to look for work," she said, to divert his attention away from her sadness.

"That you will," he replied.

"Dear Dad," Jane sighed, "he was so content with life."

Jane started work in Nichol's Animal Feeds, first in the laboratory, and later as Nutritional Advisor in Animal Husbandry. It was in this capacity she made her way to Doddsden Farm. No one returned her greeting at the dwelling house so she went over to the outhouses.

"Hello," she called out, "is this Doddsden Farm?"
"No," came the reply, "this is Dodd's Den."
John Dodds appeared in the doorway and gasped,
"Jane! It's you?"
Jane held out her hand and he shook it firmly.
"He'll probably ask me in to meet his wife," she thought sadly.
All the old feelings had come back, but she attended professionally to the business required and again held out her hand to say goodbye.
"Come on in for tea," he said, neither waiting for nor expecting a refusal.
She followed him across the yard and into the kitchen, sitting at the wooden table on the seat he proffered. They talked of student days, of who did what, and where, and when. Suddenly John asked,
"Jane, are you married?"
"No," she heard herself say, "are you?"
"No," he said quietly, and told her about his practice and the dreams he had for the farm. They laughed heartily at the ingenuous name he had given it.
They married a year later, and the years blessed them with three girls and two boys, all now married with children of their own. Jane recalled her younger son's wedding day and how she had remarked to John,
"Have you ever seen a more beautiful bride?" and how he had covered her hand with his and lovingly said,
"I have."
She turned her wedding ring on her finger and cried. Her sobs disturbed Pickles the dog. Two amber eyes appeared on her knee, followed slowly by a black body. Like John and herself, Pickles, too, was growing old. The friendship in his eyes met and held the sorrow in hers. She gently patted the head on her lap and the dog lazily shuffled his weight from her feet to his own. A sense of pins and needles prickled her legs and an overwhelming relief flooded through her. The power was coming back and she could move her legs and feet.
"Thank God," she said from the heart.
"You frightened me, Pickles," Jane scolded, but he only nuzzled closer.
"I thought, oh, never mind what I thought," she said, "its teatime."

"What did you say?" John asked from the doorway.
"Just talking to Pickles," Jane replied.

Getting There

Denis O'Sullivan

Funfair

High in the beeches the rooks screech, outraged,
as noisy preparations for the funfair challenge
their squatting rights at the fork in the road.
Tent poles cantilever skywards, urged by
bulging muscles and the profanities of straining
hands; bundles of wood and metal dragged
from lorries, transform into chair o' planes,
swingboats, helter skelter, dodgem rides;
roll a penny, find the lady, hoopla stalls,
temptingly placed to seduce the unwary.
Adrenalin-charged urchins aeroplane around
the technicoloured wagons, banking and wheeling,
heedless of danger, before setting a final course
for a decisive attack coming out of the sun.

Sugared almonds

Seven miles above the globe,
she formed the first
of many slip knots
inserted the hook and drew the yarn through,
starting a foundation chain that would encircle the earth.

I thought about Francis Chichester Clarke in Gypsy Moth IV.

High above the English Channel,
for my appraisal
she displayed the lace,
pleased at the shape, the delicate weave
eagerly cast a pretzel loop of cotton on the hook.

I read *Cloudstreet;* searching for the mood of the real Australia.

Over Rome the fifth was done,
by Singapore
she fancied thirty,
a rate of four per thousand miles,
this claim predestined to become a self-fulfilling prophecy.

I tried to count the words I'd read; lost it somewhere over Asia.

By Perth how many was in doubt
she reckoned now
in vulgar fractions
more than half the target finished -
and *still* to reach the mid-point of our circumnavigation.

I turned the pages slightly faster; I hadn't read the final chapter.

The pace to Sydney was less furious,
she luxuriated
in her satisfaction,
the backbone of the task was broken,
Melbourne, Auckland, LA, London, only twenty to be crocheted.

I should have read *Baedeker's Guide*; *Cloudstreet* wasn't very useful.

On our daughter's wedding day
each lady guest
sucked sugared almonds,
admired the lacy bags they came in,
not realising (perhaps not caring) the journey they had made to be there.

I left *Cloudstreet* on the plane; I never knew how many words per stitch.

Heron

I knew it was a heron,
even though it wasn't standing
stiffly to attention, on one leg,
in a pool, grey in the curling mist.
I did not see it spear a fish
with lightning jab, or watch
the rippling throat feathers
gloss over the engorgement.
It flapped slow, deliberate,
innocence personified,
on a gentle early morning spin,
across my breakfast view;
a gentleman taking the air
for his stomach's sake.

Looking at an old photograph

Against a white wall clothed in honeysuckle
A young boy smiles shyly, gazing at his feet,
A velvet jacket double buttoned for a coat
A school tie knotted tightly at his throat
A pair of trousers just above the knee.
A fringe of auburn hides his worried frown.
A serious business being photographed!

Rebirth

In headlong rush from mountain peaks
the melting winter snows splash
ice cold over granite, sequin speckled
pools mirroring the breaking day.
Fat willow buds sip peat brown brew,
slaking the thirst of hibernation;
primroses peek through shafts of sunlight
teasing ringleted ferns from their winter bed.
The silent forest waits, holding its breath,
straining for the trilling song of a blackbird
hidden deep in shadowy hawthorn tree.
Eruptions of spring crocus paint the earth,
Offering smiling faces to the sun,
Hopeful that the spring is here to stay.

Flying a kite

His ninth birthday present: we wrapped the red canvas
around the flimsy frame of bamboo canes, attached a
hundred metres of nylon cords securely, tied in special knots,
and walked with barely concealed anticipation round the
corner into the castle grounds.

There was just enough wind for a maiden flight.

The box soared with all the grace it could muster into
that rare space between earth and wonder, climbing
effortlessly into a sun that winked through scudding clouds.
The cord strained at full stretch as if Icarus was at its end
striving for the wild thing's freedom.

But suddenly it fell, trapped in a deadly spiral that our
frantic pulls on the loosening cords could not unwind.
Plunging now with sickening intent we saw too late
the danger that awaited. Not dashed to earth but lodged
ignominiously in a tree.

It mocks us still.

Ploughing

Bent like an anglepoise lamp
under the weight of a lifetime of toil
his hobnails echo sharp on the cobbles,
treble accompaniment to the ponderous bass
of the shire horse's hoof falls.

Shapeless tweed shrouding his shoulders
he shrugs away the morning mizzle
wrestles harness leather across the shire's
glistening chestnut back, secures the plough share
with weathered work worn hands.

Concealed behind geraniums, a tumbling
cascade, bright as blood, she watches the slow
conspiracy of man and beast trundle with
steady deliberation into the lingering wraiths
of sun glazed mist.

Jangle of brasses fades with advancing light
surrendering space to the raucous cackles of
frenzied hens, shrill squeals of restless pigs,
bawling of impatient calves, clamouring
the rattle of her stick upon the pail.

Minutes fall slowly through the sieve of time,
with floured hands she folds them into hours
measuring out the passage of the day
while he counts down the time till he returns
with every single furrow that he ploughs.

Walking by

This is the place
where violence exploded
life ended
robbed me of my
blood, my flesh,
my sanity,
my wish to live,
my humanity.
This is the place
that draws me, yet
repels me,
makes me scream
for vengeance,
for forgiveness,
release from pain,
from memory.
This is the place
I pass with eyes
that do not see,
ears that do not hear
the savagery that
scalds my brain,
grinds me into dust.
This is the place
where grief seeded
in your blood
blossomed into a
cankered rose
that sucked me dry
of the will to love
or hate.

Finger in the brain

Nothing I could have done
no question asked
no helping hand proferred
no wish conceded
no time devoted
no love bestowed.

But still the finger points
that finger in the brain.

The journeyman reaper

Scythe handle hanging loose in crooked arm,
the reaper shaves thin slivers from the plug
teases now pliant curls into the bowl.
The bellows of his cheeks cajole the fire,
smoke clouds hover in late summer air.

Spits on worn palms to embrocate the task,
bends with reverence towards the uncut grass,
sweeps the curved scythe with long and easy arc,
blade whispers, slicing through lush meadow roots
a long drawn sigh of primal husbandry.

He stops to whet the blade, with fluid grace
the stone slides hissing softly either side.
We hold our breath anticipating blood
but every stroke is sure, of practice born,
the swishing soon resumes and we relax.

Meadow shorn, scythe safely strapped aboard,
he mounts astride black Raleigh bicycle,
puffing contentedly on rekindled pipe,
rides slowly off, a brace of father's stout
to fortify him on the journey home.

Partners

Dressed in his Sunday suit, unworn for years,
a flower, red rose, in the buttonhole,
tie, striped navy, knotted by skilled hand,
handkerchief, white triangle, on his chest
black shoes, polished, planted on the floor,
gnarled fingers overlapping on his stick.

Adorned in flowered print, newly pressed,
a string of pearls, doubled round her throat,
brooch, amethyst, irridescent at her breast,
handbag, patent, mirroring on her knee,
gloves, pearl buttoned, held in tight embrace,
veined hands gently tweaking her coiffure.

Waiting, side by side they sit, apart,
Waiting for the fanfare to announce: it's
time to take your partners and make ready,
ready for the tea dance to commence.

Japanese painting

Sometimes spring catches me unawares,
like this morning, dawn chorus lingering,
I looked through glass at a full moon
in perfect symmetry with an upright cherry,
a composition of oriental formality.

Buds seemed ready to explode into life,
bringing back memories of my daughter,
haloed by double pink marshmallow blooms
cascading from the branches of another tree,
on her first communion day.

Absorbed in this Japanese painting,
fusion of orange, rose and saffron,
delicate as pashminas blown on the wind,
I'm looking at the moon,
howling inside with delight.

Another world

I live in another world.

I dwell
in shadows of days passed by
or yet to come,
like the steely dawn
unwarmed by the sun.

I linger
in the hush of words said
or about to be spoken,
like the sullen sea subsiding
from a hurricane.

I sleep
in dreams of memories gone
or still imagined,
like the grey seasons passing
through my head.

I live in another world.

Getting there

If you didn't have a pony and trap, a bicycle
was the next best thing
to get you wherever you needed to go
and back again.

An eight stone bag of meal, for the chickens,
balanced on the crossbar
a bowed leg stretched either side churning
obstinate pedals.

A small child, clinging to the handlebars, screaming
with fear and pleasure
outpacing the breezes to the bottom of the hill
and under the bridge.

A reveller, eight sheets to the wind, teetering
from verge to verge
perched precariously on wavering wheels
wobbling dangerously home.

If you didn't have a pony and trap, a bicycle
was the next best thing.

Colours
&
other stories

Denis O'Sullivan

Mary's house

The rattle of the letterbox startled Mary from her sleep.

The postman didn't come to her door very often nowadays. When Liam, her son, had bought the house from her a couple of years ago he had taken over paying the electricity, telephone and other household bills. It relieved her of much financial worry, but she missed the friendly wave of the postman and the occasional little chat on those mornings when she felt up to it.

She had dozed off in the armchair this morning beside the gas fire Liam had been good enough to instal. It was so handy not to have to worry about coal and all the mess of cleaning out the grate. As usual, Lizzie, her golden Labrador, nearly as old as herself, had barked her awake far earlier than she would have wished. Lizzie was fourteen years old now. She had been only a pup when Sean had brought her home to replace Ben, killed by a car as he tried to cross the road outside their home. Mary had thought she would never get over losing Ben and didn't really want another dog. Gradually she came to love Lizzie just as she had Ben. When Sean died a few years later, and when all the kindly well-meaning relations and friends had gone to get on with their own lives, Lizzie was there as her constant, loving companion.

Mary sometimes wondered what would become of her and Lizzie. She wasn't able to get about too well now and there were days she found it hard to look after herself, let alone Lizzie. But somehow, together, they had survived, and, in truth, they probably lived for each other as much as for themselves.

She struggled painfully from the chair. On the main road outside the house the morning traffic was thick. It was the same every day, mothers taking their kids to school, people rushing to work, delivery vans, big lorries belching diesel fumes. It hadn't been like this when Sean had carried her across the threshold of their new home nearly fifty years ago. Then it had been a quiet country road on the outskirts of a sleepy little village with the calm disturbed only by the horse traps of their neighbours and the occasional car, very much a novelty in those days. But over the years remorseless housing development had turned the village into something closer to a small town and their country lane into a busy highway with filling stations, supermarkets and an endless flow of cars and lorries, day and night.

Today was as busy as ever with the traffic lights at the end of the road punctuating the flow into a morse code of activity.

On the other side of town a burly, red-faced man sat fuming at the wheel of his shining new car, cursing and swearing at other drivers as he jostled for advantage.

"For God's sake, will you move? Why are you stopping to let him out? You're on the main road, you idiot!"

He was always impatient, but this morning things had got off to a bad start. Samantha had forgotten to iron a clean shirt for him and he had to do it himself. All day in the house with nothing else to do and she couldn't even iron his shirts. It hadn't helped when he burnt his hand on the iron. It was still smarting like hell. He'd never had that problem before he got married. His mother would have got up at dawn to make sure he had everything he needed for the day ahead.

"You have to be looking your best," she'd say. "Nobody's going to say that a son left this house without a clean shirt on his back and a good breakfast inside him."

"You're an old fusspot, ma," he'd laugh as he dashed off to work.

Mary bent slowly and picked the two letters from the mat. She heard Lizzie pawing at the door and opened it to let her in. Lizzie greeted her with as much enthusiasm as her advanced years would allow.

"There, there, old girl. Don't get yourself excited. We're well past that."

She looked around for her reading glasses but couldn't find them. It was always the same; she would take them off and leave them down and then couldn't remember where she had left them. She consoled herself that it was just one other aspect of growing old but she sometimes worried that it might be something more serious. She was always meaning to get one of those chain things so that she could hang the spectacles round her neck, but she kept forgetting about it when she was out shopping. Eventually she found the glasses on the arm of her chair and, putting them on, glanced at the letter in the gold envelope, promises of free gifts printed on it. She set it aside to read later, never liking to throw such letters out too quickly, just in case!

Eagerly she looked at the handwriting on the other letter. It appeared familiar but she couldn't think at first whose it might be. Adjusting her glasses she realised the letter was from Liam.

"My goodness! What could Liam be writing to us about, Lizzie?"

She ruffled the labrador's head absent-mindedly, thinking fondly of her only son.

"It's a long time since Liam wrote to us."

Her thoughts drifted back to a time many years ago when he was away in England working for Wimpey. He wrote to tell them he was engaged to a girl called Samantha and they were going to get married very soon. Mary and Sean were upset he hadn't brought Samantha home to meet them first even though they had grown used to Liam's impulsiveness. But they had been bitterly disappointed when he had telephoned two weeks later to say he and Samantha were already married and they would come home on a visit as soon as they could get away. It had taken three years for them to make the trip and by then Sean was in the final stages of his long fight against cancer. Lizzie flopped down beside the chair as Mary went for a knife to slit open the envelope.

He reached the office in a foul mood. Within twenty minutes he had managed to reduce his secretary to tears. She was locked, weeping, in the ladies' toilet causing intense cross-legged embarrassment to the office junior.

The Sales Manager hurried stony faced from the office, fired for the third time that month.

Inside, he sat at his desk, head in hands. He couldn't take much more of this. When he had taken over the family construction business after his father's death it had been a small, thriving concern. His father had been content to spend his life doing modest building jobs, houses for local people, sheds, repair work. He had never strayed far from the part of the country where he had grown up, where he was known and liked by the people he worked for. Liam had no time for that. He wanted to have one of the biggest construction companies in Ireland instead of shilly-shallying around with footling little jobs for country yokels. And, in the course of the last few years, he had made many enemies in his ruthless pursuit of that goal. He was feeling the effects of that now with two near certain contracts lost in as many weeks, due, he suspected, to deliberate undercutting by a rival firm. And now the bank manager was on the phone practically every day.

"Just a courtesy call, Mr. Maguire. I was wondering how those new contracts were coming along. Head Office, you know, they won't let us get on with things in our own way these days."

He felt like telling him to stuff the overdraft but his instinct for self-survival prevented him. If only he could get his hands on the money from the house it would give him a bit of breathing space. When he had bought it the business had been doing very well and it didn't occur to him that he would have to resort to selling the house before the old girl passed on. Quite simply, he had considered the purchase as a sound investment at a time when prices were reasonable. Since then they had gone through the roof; the house would sell for three times what he had paid for it. But it wouldn't be worth much to him if he couldn't get rid of it soon. Only he knew that he had bought the house with the firm's money. If the company went to the wall the receivers would get their hands on the house as well.

Mary's hand trembled as she slipped the single sheet of notepaper from the envelope. Unfolding it she held it up to the light so that she could make out Liam's hurried scrawl on the page, and, smiling, started to read. As she read, the smile was replaced at first by a puzzled frown, and then, slowly, the words on the page dissolved into a blur as tears started to roll down her cheeks.

"Oh! My God, Lizzie, he wants me to go into a home. I can't believe it. Liam wouldn't do that to me."

She grasped the arm of the chair to steady herself as she searched for her handkerchief in the sleeve of her cardigan.

"He told me I could stay here for as long as I needed it."

Lizzie rose, placing her head on Mary's knee. The old lady looked at the dog with her head bowed, still weeping.

"What's to become of us, Lizzie, what's to become of us?"

Liam picked up the phone. He couldn't wait any longer; he had to know if he was going to be able to raise the money on the house. He hadn't thought about what he was going to say to his mother but he had to talk to her. She would have got the letter by now. The sooner he got things moving the better. It would be a bit of a shock for her but he felt sure she would see the sense of it. She was always so sensible.

The phone rang and rang. He waited, drumming the fingers of his free hand on the desk, his rising irritation apparent as he waited for it to be answered. The ringing stopped and he leaned forward, anxious to get the conversation over with, but all he heard was the familiar voice of his mother on the answering service saying,

"Mary is unable to answer your call at present but please leave your name and number...."

He slammed the instrument down in disgust, instantly recoiling with the pain as his temporarily forgotten burnt hand struck the cradle of the telephone.

"Where is she? Surely to God she can't be out at this hour of the morning."

Lizzie barked and rose to a sitting position when she heard the phone ringing, looking up at Mary slumped in the chair beside her, wet handkerchief still held tightly in her hand. When Mary didn't respond Lizzie nuzzled her and whined trying to attract her attention.

Colours

On the night I moved in here those wee slabbers from the big houses on the other side of the park smashed every bloody window. When all the glass was gone, they moved on, probably to annoy some other poor bastard.

I've been here two months. I'm getting used to all the crap around me, but it's not as bad as the last kip where the rain came in everywhere and even the heaviest cardboard didn't survive one wet night. At least this place still has a roof.

The board outside says "Exclusive development of 2 and 3 room apartments built to the highest standards with every possible amenity".

Each day, I expect to see the workmen with their Bob the Builder hats and Scoop and Dump arriving to pull the place apart. That would put me back on the street. My mates as well; well, two of them are mates, that frigger Lefty can rot in hell for all I care. If he'd leave me alone it would be alright but we didn't hit it off from the start; not after I told him I didn't do drugs or glue. He wouldn't believe it, thought I was holding out on him. Now he needles me all the time, always wanting his share, even though he wouldn't give you the snot from his nose. A right swine, especially with a load on, when he decides he's going to have a bit of fun, in other words knocking the tar out of me or some other miserable sod. Mean bastard, red bloated face, wee piggy eyes, huge hairy arms with a tattoo of SUSIE pulsing across an obscene red heart. He must have been at sea or something; pity he hadn't done the decent thing and fallen overboard when he had the chance.

The first time he hit me I wasn't expecting it. Well, I was pissed and so was he and we were fooling around. I thought he was a mate and all. You don't expect a mate to have a go at you. Pat and Jimmy dragged him off before he could do a proper job. Bloody lucky for me they were there.

"You stole my fags, you wee shit," he roared, "I'll kill you."

Jimmy was hanging from his left arm, Pat from his right; they were having a hell of a job holding him back. From the look on his face I knew he was in earnest so I didn't stick around.

When I snuck back a few hours later he was sleeping off the Magners in a corner where I usually bedded down; but who was arguing? One dig in the jaw is enough. I'm a fast learner. I'd be keeping well out of his way in future.

Next morning he was all over me.

"I'm sorry, ach, I'm so sorry, Mickey. I didn't mean it. Honest to God, I'll never hit you again. It was the drink talking. Come on, be a pal, shake on it."

I wasn't keen, pals like him I could do without. But he banged on about it so much I got fed up listening to him.

"OK, OK. We'll forget about it."

He insisted on shaking hands. I enjoyed seeing him wince when I put a wee bit of extra pressure on, just for luck, although I'm sure his knuckles didn't hurt as much as my jaw. Later, gazing at my reflection in a shop window in Botanic Avenue, I could see the left side of my face badly swollen and a big blue bruise beginning to show through the scraggy beard - what I used to call my designer stubble.

After that, things were alright for a while, apart from the usual problems you have when you're living on the streets. It was a sight different from the weekly shop with Sharon at the supermarket, before she threw me out, that is. No loading up the trolley now; more a case of a nightly rummage through the bins behind the restaurants and shops - you'd be surprised how much stuff gets dumped every day. Even so it was a while before I was able to bring myself to fighting for the better bits with the local strays and the occasional fox. The rats I tried not to think about.

When I found a whole chicken one night I could barely believe my luck. Wiping away a few globs of coleslaw and lettuce with the sleeve of my anorak, I sunk my teeth into it. Jesus, the taste brought the memories rushing back – Sharon, clean clothes, good food. With the first pangs of hunger satisfied, sticking the remainder of the chicken inside my coat, I ran back to the building, ready to enjoy a leisurely feast. Ducking through the hole in the fence, I drooled at the thought of the pleasure ahead and practically bounced off Lefty, standing just inside, legs straddling a pool of dirty water, Belfast's unshaven answer to the Colossus of Rhodes.

"What's your hurry; can you not watch where you're going?"

I could see he'd been on the booze again. The face was flushed and the wee hard bloodshot eyes drilled into me. I turned to run but wasn't quick enough to avoid the cruel hand that clamped onto my arm.

"What have you got there? Trying to hide something?" He slurred, dragging me closer until our faces were just inches apart. I turned my head to avoid the foul breath as he ripped my anorak open and spotted the chicken.

"You greedy wee bastard. A whole chicken and you're not going to give your mate a bit." He backhanded me hard across the face. As I lay in a heap at his feet, he kicked me half a dozen times in the ribs for good measure. It's a mercy he had the chicken to worry about or he might have forgotten to stop kicking.

I can't remember where I spent that night. Pat and Jimmy were away in a squat across town for a few days so there was nobody to protect me when Lefty finished with the chicken. I had to get away from him before he decided to have a bit more fun. Like an injured animal I sought refuge to lick my wounds and live through the night, and the next day and the next.

But I didn't forget.

When I got a chance I examined the bruises, peeling the layers of filthy clothing from my body to reveal big ugly patches, purple and blue and red and yellow, a spectrum of pain spreading across and through my body. My jaw hurt like hell; I didn't need the shop window this time to show me the colour of the bruises. The rainbow of agony etched itself into my brain, never allowing me to forget what that big fucker had done to me, and worse, what he might have done if he hadn't been so anxious to get at the chicken.

I stayed well away from him after that, returning only to sleep at the house, always disappearing into my bolt hole at the first sign that he had been on the drink. Like a battered wife I lived in constant dread of my tormentor but couldn't make the break that would start to solve the problem.

When you've been expecting something for a long time and it doesn't materialise, it can be a big surprise, a shock even, when it happens. That's how it was when the builders came eventually to knock the house down. The first I knew of it was doors banging, the racket of heavy machine engines revving and a lot of shouting going on outside. I peeped cautiously over the sill, ducking down abruptly to avoid the gaze of the crane driver perched high in his orange cab. Gathering my stuff together, I slipped quietly out the back door into the alley. By the time I'd made it round to the front and positioned myself on the other side of the street, the demolition ball was already swinging. With every pass the width of the arc widened, the ball gleaming dimly in the autumn sunlight as it closed by degrees on its target. I stayed just long enough to see the first glorious, spectacular strike. The whole front wall collapsed in a churning mass of bricks bringing the gable wall with it, sending up great clouds of dust mingled with the cheers of the small band of spectators and workmen.

The last I saw was the JCB moving in to gouge up the fallen mountain of bricks and rotting timber, disgorging it onto the waiting lorries.

I ran until I could run no more, falling against a lamppost, dragging air into my rebelling lungs. All I could see were the colours, colours everywhere. I pulled my Bennie hat down over my eyes, and navigating by the lines between the pavers, I walked straight off the kerb. Raucous sounds of car horns, squeal of brakes, angry shouts, the colours dancing and leaping, exhilarating, charged with danger. I ripped the hat off my head and ran like a maniac back across the road, flailing at the colours with my hat. But the colours were still there, in my head, in my brain, forever changing, confusing, swirling round and round, blue and purple and red and yellow clouds on a weather map of emotions, the colours of the bruises on Lefty, lying under the bricks of the demolished house.

They laugh with me; the frigging colours laugh with me.

Mother's attic

Ellie poked her head through the trapdoor opening and groaned at the chaos in the roofspace. She had known, ever since the death of her mother two months earlier, that at some point she would have to face the prospect of clearing out the loft. She had shied away from the task for as long as possible. But now, with the house sold, and the new owners expecting to move in a week today, the job was urgent.

Stacks of boxes covered the floor. Only a few could be identified – the box for the computer her Dad had bought just a year before he died, the packaging of the DVD player she had bought her Mammy for Christmas. She wondered aloud why they hadn't been thrown out but knew, at the same time, that her parents never discarded anything that might "come in useful" in the future.

"What in the name of all that's holy am I going to do with this pile of stuff?" she muttered, as she heaved herself up and stood surveying the mess; "It'll take a month to sort it all out."

She had hoped to work her way carefully through the contents of the attic, the remains of her parents' lives, sifting the good from the bad, deciding what to keep, what to send to the charity shop or the auction and what to dump.

"There's no way I'll be able to do anything other than to chuck the whole lot out."

It was not how she had imagined it. She had seen herself sorting lovingly through things last touched by her parents, treasuring the nostalgic remembrances of the two people she had loved most in all the world. A tear trickled down her cheek. She wiped it away brusquely.

"Come on now, girl. Nothing else for it, better make a start."

A lot of the boxes she lifted at first were empty, apart from the polythene bags and pieces of polystyrene that had been the original wrappings for the new TV, DVD, food mixer, Dyson vacuum cleaner and the motley collection of household bric-a-brac accumulated over the years. As she chucked them through the trap onto the landing and the pile mounted, Ellie began to feel a bit more optimistic about the job.

She gauged the vacant area with her eye.

"I'll do just a few more boxes and then I'll stop and have a wee cup of tea."

As she began to pull the next box towards her she knew it wasn't empty.

"Oh, well it had to happen sooner or later. I'll have to open this one and see what's in it. With a bit of luck it'll be a load of old garbage I can bin."

The box was covered in a fine veneer of dust. She stripped the brown parcel tape away and raised the lid. Puzzled, she stared at the numerous neatly wrapped packages, recognizing the careful work of her mother's hands. The topmost package, bigger than the rest, was not as heavy as she expected. She paused, steadying herself, worried that she might be about to violate some private area her parents had not shared with her.

As the wrapping paper fell to the floor, she stared at the little figure, taking in the knitted baby clothes and the bandage wound around his left arm, the bandage she had put there fifty years ago when Teddy had been a patient in the dolls' hospital. She had no idea that her mother had kept him. And now, as she wept anew for her mother, she clasped Teddy to her breast, feeling the familiar comfort of him, smelling the peculiar TCP aroma that had lingered ever since she had secretly vaccinated him against measles.

Hijack

Eight o'clock, a dark miserable night, and he was on his way home at last.

Allowing the old Peugeot to coast down the Crumlin Road on autopilot, he tried to rid his mind of all the shit that had happened in the last twenty four hours. The riots the night before had left the usual trail of distraught mothers with small children hanging on their skirts, wide eyed with lack of sleep. Most were too afraid to go back to their homes; he had spent hours with local community representatives and social workers trying to fix them up with places to stay.

Sometimes, he wondered if he was cut out for this type of work. The endless succession of pitiful faces, victims of sectarian strife, drained him. He cursed the self-styled freedom fighters who brought this sorrow on their own communities; a handful of psychopaths, they didn't care who got hurt or how much damage they did, so long as they got their kicks. And worst of all he hated the way they used the youngsters to do their dirty work for them.

As Brookfield Mill slipped by in the deepening gloom, he spotted a dark figure standing in the road immediately ahead. Slamming on the brakes he slithered to a halt mere yards short of the upraised arm. Too late he spotted the balaclava. A second figure ran from the side of the road and stuck a revolver through the partially open window.

"We're taking yer car, mate."

"For God's sake, give us a break. I've been up all night trying to sort people out after last night's trouble."

"Get out now and you won't get hurt. The army needs this car. Leave the keys in her."

Michael opened the door and stepped into the road.

"See that door over there? Wait in there for twenty minutes. Don't look back."

He turned from the middle of the road and heard the car engine being gunned and the squeal of tyres as it took off towards the city centre. As he pushed on the door he became aware of a small crowd of children gathering up the road.

"Fuck, they're taking big Duggan's car."

The ribald laughter mocked him as he moved slowly into the dim light, realising that he was in a shebeen. As he ventured closer, he could see that the place was like any normal public house with an extensive range of beers and spirits on display behind the well stocked bar. The only difference was the semi darkness of the remainder of the room where he could barely see the tables set well back from the bar. The barman approached.

"Haven't seen you here before mate, have I?" Michael wasn't sure if he detected a note of menace in the voice.

"I've just lost my car. Two guys took it off me out on the road there. They told me to wait here for twenty minutes."

It was only now that Michael sensed the presence of others in the bar, as the hum of voices started up behind him.

"Well, I suppose I might as well have a pint of Guinness while I'm waiting."

'No problem, mate. Ye'd be needing one."

As things turned out he needed two. The first one disappeared in record time amidst a mixture of shock and relief.

He was three quarters way through the second when the door burst open. A hand threw something onto the bar.

"Yer car's down the road at the picture house."

The noise of the slamming door reverberated off the low ceiling as the keys skidded to a halt beside Michael's nearly empty glass.

"Right, mate, there ye go. You must be one of the lucky ones." The barman didn't suggest another drink.

Only as Michael neared home did it occur to him that the car could well have been booby trapped while in the hands of the hijackers. Sweat trickled down his face as he stopped the car on the Cavehill Road. Even after he had satisfied himself that there was nothing there, he stood for several minutes trembling.

"Christ, the thought of it. They could have done anything to this motor. I could be all over the road by now. God, I'll not do that again."

He didn't venture into the Ardoyne for several days, needing to rest his shattered nerves for a while before going into the field again. But even so, it was surprising how quickly he found himself immersed once more in the endless stream of troubles created by the warring factions.

At the end of a particularly difficult day, some months after the hijacking, a community leader he had been working with suggested a pint.

"Where would you get a pint at this hour? It's one o'clock in the morning."

"Don't ask," tapping the side of his nose with a dirty finger, "just leave it up to yer Uncle Tommy. He'll see ye right."

Tommy led the way through a maze of side streets that Michael had difficulty recognising in the dismal half light of the few scattered street lights that had escaped the attentions of the Brits and the RA. They arrived eventually at what seemed to be a blank wall. Tommy rapped sharply on a hardly visible door, three short knocks, pause, one knock, pause, then two more. The door opened briefly and was closed quickly behind them.

"Who have you there, Tommy?" The voice, deep, suspicious, came from the darkness at the back of the narrow hallway.

"Ach, its just big Michael. He's a mate. We've been hard at it all day cleaning up after them bastards from the other side. We need a pint bad."

"Right, Tommy, away ye go." A door opened, the light from inside relieving the gloom in the hall for long enough to let them enter. Michael could see the sweep of the bar with its brightly coloured optics and shining glasses. Shadows concealed the patrons seated at the tables in the rear. Only when he advanced further and recognised the barman did he realise he was in the shebeen where he had waited on the night his car was hijacked.

He stood at the bar with Tommy waiting for the two pints they had ordered. The barman showed no sign of recognition as he slid the glasses of foaming black stout towards them.

"Take it out o' that." Tommy slid a tenner across the bar.

"They're paid for." The barman pushed the note back to Tommy and turned away.

Michael returned the untouched pint to the counter. He spoke loudly.

"I don't drink unless I know who's paying."

The room hushed; Tommy's glass froze in mid-air half way to his mouth. Feet shuffled in the shadows. A voice from the back of the room broke the silence.

"Will that cover the cost of the petrol for the night we borrowed yer car, big fella?"

Michael raised the glass to his lips and drained it in one. Signalling the barman he said,

"I'll have another one of those, wherever it came from."

Not at this address

Martha pushed open the door, tut-tutting with annoyance as it jammed against the pile of mail lying behind it.

"Good Lord, where does all this junk come from?" she flustered as the alarm beeped urgently. Balancing the small box of groceries she carried in one hand, she struggled to key in the code, breathing her usual sigh of relief when the alarm's urgent signal stopped. She pushed the front door shut with her foot, pressed down the handle of the kitchen door with an elbow, and, as it swung open, dumped the carton of groceries unceremoniously onto the worktop. Not stopping to remove her coat, she dashed for the bathroom.

Returning to the kitchen, she threw the coat over a chair and held the spout of the electric kettle under the cold tap, careful not to put too much water in.

"No point in wasting money," she muttered, as always, a hint of pride in her attention to this small detail of home economics. "Pat would have filled it to the top, silly old fool." It didn't matter how often she told him, he never seemed to learn.

"It'll be the sorry day when we can't afford a drop of hot water for the tae," he would say. "Sure you never know who might drop in."

She often spoke to herself as if Pat was still there. Habit, she consoled herself, that was all. When he was alive it didn't matter too much about the odd bit of waste, but now was different. She had to watch the pennies. Not like her sister-in-law, Margaret, up the road. Pat's brother, John, had been a prosperous builder and had left Margaret well off when he had passed on.

It was then she remembered the mail lying in the hall. She bent to pick up the gaudily coloured envelopes, offers of free this and free that, with "THIS IS NOT A CIRCULAR" printed across some of them. As she turned to go back into the kitchen the bell rang, startling her. In her haste to get the key from the porcelain bowl on the hall table she dropped all the letters. The key wasn't in the bowl.

"Hello, Mrs. Rafferty, are you there?"

She recognized the voice of her next door neighbour, that old busybody, Sarah O'Reilly.

"Did you know you left your keys in the front door?" the neighbour continued.

Martha slapped her hand to her forehead as she swung the

door open.

"I'd forget my head if it wasn't screwed on," she thought, remembering that she had been in such a rush to silence the alarm that she had left the key in the lock

"Ah sure I was just leaving my shopping into the kitchen. I couldn't manage the keys as well. I was in the hall ready to open the door to get them when you rang the bell. Well, thanks very much anyway."

"None of us is getting any younger, Martha. Didn't I forget to let the dog in the other night. The poor ould thing was sitting on the front step all wet and shaking like a leaf when I went out to get the milk in the next morning. You should have seen the look he gave me. It took me two hours to get him dried and warmed up."

Sarah moved forward as if to step through the open door. But Martha, determined not to have to stand listening to Sarah's tittle tattle, muttered "I'll talk to you later, Sarah, I haven't got time just now."

She closed the door firmly, turning the key in the lock, and leaned against it, playing absent mindedly with the pearl brooch pinned to the lapel of her woollen cardigan. Pat had given her the brooch soon after they had met. Touching it always helped; it was as if Pat was there saying, "Keep calm now, Martha. Don't be getting all excited."

"That's all I need - that nosey old so and so to be telling everybody I'm getting forgetful. They'll be thinking I'm not fit to look after myself next."

She stooped to retrieve the letters from the floor and only then noticed the slim cream envelope. Placing the rest of the pile on the table, she examined the letter more closely. The envelope looked expensive, not like the flimsy air mail letters that she got occasionally from her daughter in America. Turning it over she was surprised to see that the sender's name and address was that of a large local firm of solicitors.

"What in the name of heavens can a solicitor be writing to me about?" Martha was mystified. Pat's will had been cleared up long ago and even that hadn't involved this particular firm.

Martha's hands shook as she ripped the letter open. It was brief and very much to the point.

Dear Mrs. Rafferty,

We are writing to advise you that as the only surviving relative of your late aunt, Rebecca Donnelly, who passed away in Australia some 2 years ago, you are the sole beneficiary of her will. The enclosed cheque in the sum of £6,500 represents the full and final amount due to you.

We regret the delay in contacting you but you will appreciate that in the circumstances it was necessary to establish the identity and whereabouts of Mrs. Donnelly's surviving relatives before our duty in this matter could be discharged.

Please sign the acknowledgement of receipt and return to this office in the enclosed postpaid envelope.

Yours sincerely,
Thomas Johnson Jnr
Senior Partner.

Confused, Martha looked at the cheque. It was made out to her, Mrs. M. Rafferty.

"But, who was Rebecca Donnelly? I don't know any Rebecca Donnelly. I don't remember an Aunt Rebecca."

She sat down in a chair, all thoughts of tea forgotten.

"I don't understand this. My father didn't have any sisters and my mother's sisters were Alice and Mary. Where could this Aunt Rebecca have come from?"

She gazed in puzzlement at the cheque in her hand.

"But this cheque is made out to me."

Then the truth struck her like a thunderbolt. "Oh, no, don't let it be true. Please, please, don't let it be true."

Her anxiety mounted as she looked frantically around the kitchen for the envelope the letter had come in. She eventually realized it was clenched tightly in her other hand. Smoothing it out on the table she read her name and then the address. As far as she could make out it was addressed to her, her name, her house number, her street, her town. She carried the envelope to the window to get a better look and only then realized that the stylized lettering had confused her; the house number was 477, not 277.

Her worst fears had come true; the letter should have gone to her sister-in-law, Margaret, not her. Now she vaguely remembered having heard that Margaret's mother had a younger sister called Rebecca who had emigrated to Australia many years ago. Whatever had been the cause of Rebecca's departure, nobody in her family talked about it; as far as they were concerned poor Rebecca might as well have never existed. That was why she hadn't recognized the name Donnelly; Rebecca must have married out in Australia.

"That Margaret one," Martha wailed, "with her big car and her foreign holidays and fancy clothes, what does she need more money for? And here I am with hardly tuppence to spare at the end o' the week." The tears flowed freely, the injustice of it all too much to bear.

Martha took a long time to compose herself.

"Ah, sure, as long as we have enough to get by on, what more do we need?" Pat's often repeated words came back to her as she struggled into her recently discarded coat. But this time they did nothing to console her.

"Best go up there and get it over and done with," she sniffed, rubbing at her reddened eyes with the corner of a tissue.

As she waited at the bus stop, Martha brooded on just how unfair life could be. What could she not have done with that money? Margaret would probably blow it on another cruise or swanning around with one of her toy boys. For her, Martha, it would be the difference between living from hand to mouth and having a "wee bit of roughness to come and go on" as Pat used to say.

She saw the bus easing into the traffic from the stop down the road. As it pulled into the kerb in front of her, doors swooshing open, she hesitated. The driver looked at her questioningly,

"Here, missus, I can't wait all day. Make up your mind."

Martha regarded him through red-rimmed eyes and started to move towards the bus. Then she stopped abruptly as if she had just remembered something important she had to do, stepped away from the stop, waving the driver to go on and turned back in the direction of her home.

This time she made sure to remove the keys from the door before she turned off the alarm. She needed time to herself and certainly didn't want Sarah O'Reilly anywhere near her just now. If she had offended Sarah earlier, and she was sure she had, she could always invite her in for a cup of tea another day and apologise then. She couldn't afford to be distracted when she had serious thinking to do. Here was an opportunity and she wasn't going to waste it by making up her mind too quickly. What was it Pat always said? Aye, that was it, "act in haste, repent at leisure."

Martha made herself a nice strong cup of tea and, as she sipped it, read the letter again. She looked at the cheque, her hand trembling as she thought of just what she could do with that much money. It was the sort of amount that somebody with Margaret's money wouldn't even miss but to her it represented a small fortune. She would be able to afford an occasional trip to the bingo or to the theatre. She could enjoy a cup of tea and a cream cake in a restaurant after she had done her meagre weekly shopping instead of always scrimping and saving to eke out her small pension. Indeed, she might even be able to treat herself to those expensive chocolate chip cookies that Pat always liked so much. And, in any case, Margaret didn't even know about Aunt Rebecca's missing legacy. Didn't the solicitor say in the letter he had been looking for her for the past two years?

What's more hadn't the family done everything possible to ensure that Rebecca wasn't even so much as a distant memory? Margaret would no more be expecting a legacy from her than would Martha herself.

Her mind in turmoil, Martha failed to notice the light passing and it was with a start that she saw it was long past her usual bedtime.

As she knelt by the side of her bed to say her prayers, she held Pat's memorial card. The passing years had done little to diminish the sense of hurt and loss but she always managed to regain something of the companionship they had shared by gazing at his photograph. But tonight, she could hardly bear to look into his eyes. She could sense the disapproving expression she would find there.

Martha knew what Pat would have done and now she was sure of what she must do.

"Good night, Pat," she murmured, "I'll go to see Margaret first thing in the morning."

After the funeral

After the funeral the mourners gathered in Moran's public house. The creamy pints of Guinness and golden balls of malt soon dispelled the bone numbing coldness of the cemetery and the solemn demeanour of the occasion.

John Walsh stood at the bar with a group of men, head tilted first this way then the other, as he graciously acknowledged expressions of condolences on the death of his father.

"Ah, sure he had a good innings, eighty nine wasn't it?" Mickey Devine spoke with unaccustomed reverence.

"Thanks, Mickey. A good stretch indeed."

Far too bloody long, he thought, *nearly took the farm with him.*

Paddy Brennan spoke, the glass of stout halfway to his lips: "Ach, a better more Christian man never walked the earth. He would have done anything for you."

"He would that," rejoined Mickey, not wanting to be upstaged by a guttersnipe like Paddy Brennan. "I remember when I had that wee spot o' bother with the police over the drop of poitin they found in the barn, sure didn't he speak up for me and not a word said?"

"He would always speak up for a neighbour, Mickey. He would never be found lacking."

John took a pull on the pint. *Why wouldn't he speak up, and him pickled in the bloody stuff.*

Paddy spoke again. "Well now, that's as maybe, Mickey, but there's many's a one could say the same. Like when my ould horse fell dead between the shafts yon day didn't he let me have one of his for next to nothing. Man I was glad of that. I don't know what I would have done without it."

"Aye, generous to a fault."

John nodded to Paddy. *The ould horse was dying on its feet. He couldn't have got rid at any price except to an ould fool like you, Paddy Brennan.*

"Another round there, Liam, when you're ready," John shouted above the din. The stocky publican began to pull the pints, his moon face glowing with the heat and the regular half 'uns of Powers he concealed behind the bar. "The ould fellow would have enjoyed a wee do like this. He'll be sorry he's missing it."

Liam smiled. "He didn't like to miss giving a neighbour a good send off, now, Liam, that's true." *A pretty penny you made out of him, ye miserable git. Sending him home full to beat the crap outa me ma.*

"A good husband and father, he was now, none better. There's not one around here would say different. No, not a one." Liam spoke with authority, heads nodding around him in affirmation.

"Well, now, that's very nice of you to say that. May both of their souls rest in peace." John made the sign of the cross on his forehead.

May that ould bastard rot in hell, he thought.

"I suppose you'll be keeping on the farm, John?" The new voice was that of Robbie Toner, a big farmer from the neighbouring parish.

"Well, Robbie, to tell the truth, I haven't given it much thought yet. I'll need to get my head cleared before I'll be fit to see what has to be done."

You'll not be getting it anyway, ye greedy swine. Ye'd rob the dead if you thought you'd get away with it.

"Ah, sure, now's not the time to be talking about things like that. Your father would never have sold the place. I made him a good offer for it more than once. But, he wasn't for budging." Robbie sucked his pipe, a faraway look in his eye. "We'll all miss him, a fine man, salt o' the earth."

"You never said a truer word."

John smiled as Robbie turned away. *You wouldn't know the truth if it jumped up and bit ye.*

"John, John, there you are." The tones of the Parish Priest were unmistakeable. John smiled, the Guinness suddenly turning to acid in his stomach.

Aw Holy God! Here comes Whispering Jesus. It's going to be a long night.

The money tree

"Sarah. James. Come along, quickly now, into the Volvo."

Robbie heard Caroline, crisp and businesslike, urging the children, anxious to leave.

He didn't know why she always said 'Volvo' instead of 'car'. You would think they'd a fleet of limousines to choose from rather than just the three-year old Volvo that was beginning to show the effects of his lack of interest. Unlike some of the neighbours, he wasn't out there every Sunday acting as if washing the car was a surer way to heaven than going to church. Not that he went to church himself. He couldn't be bothered with any of that stuff now. His parents used to make him go three times on Sunday when he was a kid so he reckoned he had a few brownie points to call on.

Outside, the car door slammed. He listened to the receding note of the engine as it disappeared down the park. They lived in a park now. He had to admit their house was a hell of a sight better than anything he had ever expected to own. If it had been left to him they would probably still be living in a council estate with paramilitary flags on every lamppost and red, white and blue kerbstones along the footpath. When he'd carried her over the threshold after they came back from the honeymoon in Tenerife, Caroline had taken one look and said,

"It'll do for a start."

She said that about everything - car, house, furniture, everything. He supposed she must have been saying it long before they got married, but he'd never noticed it. When they started going out together he'd loved the way she was so decisive, always full of plans.

"We'll go for a nice meal first and then we can nip down to Capronis for a bit of a twirl," she would say. He was only too glad to be doing something that she wanted.

In the early days of marriage he loved to please Caroline; she could ask anything and he would do his damnedest to get it for her. Not that she ever asked too much, it was always something that he could deliver with just a wee bit of extra effort, a few hours overtime and, later on, when he got into the sales game, just one more call.

She used to say,

"Robbie! I can hardly wait to see you moving to something better than that dead end job you're in at the minute. You're far too good to spend all your days at that boring old job. Mark my words, there's somebody out there who'll appreciate you much more. One of these days..."

The unfinished sentence would hang in the air between them like a promise. Or she'd look across the table at him, a wistful look in her beautiful blue eyes,

"Wouldn't it be wonderful to move to a better neighbourhood where we would have a little bit of a garden and suitable friends for the kids. We could maybe even have a decent car and be able to afford holidays in the sun. Maybe even buy an apartment in Spain eventually."

He was happy to go along with her. He loved the feeling that he was capable of anything, provided he knew what she wanted. And there was nobody could match him at the selling, not even that poncy bastard Perkins with his fancy degrees and marketing diplomas. When it came to a head to head on the road he could outsell him every time.

But he found it hard to get enthusiastic about climbing the career ladder. He didn't want the responsibility; he always needed a bit of encouragement to change anything.

He liked the way Caroline tried to do the best for the kids but he didn't want to see them turn into a couple of wee snobs with snotty voices and high faluting ways about them. Not that Caroline was a snob but she wanted them to have the best of everything. He did, too; but he didn't see how spending an extra twenty quid on a school uniform or a pair of trainers was going to make a lot of difference, especially when it was only a few weeks before the expensive ones looked just as grubby as the cheaper gear. Ah, bugger it, anyway; sure he was earning good money as a sales rep with Mooney's. What's twenty quid here or there? If it hadn't been for Caroline he would still be travelling the country in O'Reilly's van trying to flog fancy goods to wee sweetie shops instead of doing big money deals with some of the largest property developers and builders in the country. He owed that to her; she knew what he was capable of better than he did himself.

Two years ago, while he was still working for O'Reilly, he heard there was a sales job going at Mooney's. He didn't want to apply but Caroline had different ideas.

"'Oh, don't be stupid, Robbie. Why are you always underselling yourself?"

He said nothing. Caroline was adept at questions that he

didn't have to answer.

"You're just as good as anybody else. Go in there and tell them how much business you did out of that old van for O'Reilly last year. Tell them they'll be making a big mistake not to give you a chance."

She looked at him, brow furrowed, as if puzzled that he couldn't see that.

"Anyway, you should try to better yourself even if it's only for the sake of the kids."

And, lo and behold, he had got the job and now here he was with a company car -the Volvo - a good salary and, even better, a healthy commission every time he managed to persuade a builder to use Mooney's products.

He enjoyed the new job and after a while he was glad that he had made the move from O'Reilly's. Nonetheless, he wondered sometimes if he was being sucked into a life he didn't really want, as if he was trapped in a web that he hadn't spun and that he couldn't escape from.

And, now, it was happening again.

Just last week, on the way home from one of their rare outings without the kids, he'd tried to explain to Caroline why he didn't want to apply for the vacant Sales Manager job at Simpson's.

"Look, Caroline,"' he said, "we've got a grand house and car, two lovely kids and a couple of trips to Spain every year. What more do we need?"

"I know, Robbie darling, we're very lucky really. But you're so good at what you do that I just hate to see people like that Harry Perkins getting promotion ahead of you. Mooney's aren't treating you too well at the moment. You deserve better. I think you should go for the Sales Manager job at Simpson's. It's not the money or anything but you would have less travelling to do and a bigger car."

"Why would I want to be a Sales Manager? It's only a load of extra hassle trying to get other guys to meet targets so you can get a decent bonus yourself. And we already have a good car. There's plenty more miles in that Volvo. It's top of the range and its only coming up on three years old."

"Oh, that old thing!" She dismissed the Volvo with an airy wave. "Harry has a nice new BMW and Marion says it's absolutely lovely. I can just see you behind the wheel; it would suit you so much better than Harry. He hasn't the build for it."

Robbie groaned; just when he was well settled into the job

with Mooney's, looking forward to taking it a bit easier, she was dragging him up the social ladder again. That was the trouble. Caroline had always been on a higher rung, looking up to see how many steps there were to the top. He'd never bothered; he'd always wanted to settle where he was, content with familiar situations and people he'd known all his life. He didn't want to make changes that meant having to make new friends. He hated all that small talk and pretending to enjoy the gossip that passed for intelligent conversation. He'd rather have a few pints with his old mates any day.

But he knew that there would be no rest until he moved on. The kids were doing well at school but they would soon be going to the Grammar and that would involve a lot more keeping up. That's what Caroline would want, no doubt about it. And, of course, you can't leave the kids off to school in anything less than a BMW these days. He wouldn't mind but the little buggers were as bad as Caroline, always wanting new things. What the Hell is the world coming to, he thought darkly, all these modern youngsters turning up their noses unless Daddy's got a BMW or a Mercedes? In his day, he bloody well walked to school and was lucky to have a jam sandwich in his school bag for his lunch. Too many TV ads; they thought money grew on trees. Except Caroline, of course, she thought he was the money tree.

In the end, he applied for the job at Simpson's, Caroline had seen to it, but he had already decided that he wasn't going to try too hard. If he didn't get it he could always argue that he wasn't up to management. Surely Caroline would see the sense of that.

The interviews had been a few days ago and he had come away quietly confident that he hadn't got the job.

"It went fine," he said, when Caroline asked about the interview.

"What sort of things did they ask you?" she persisted.

"Oh, you know all the usual things. Where I had worked before and what sort of targets I had and whether or not I met them." He was deliberately vague.

There were three of them on the panel, old John Simpson himself, the Personnel man, whom Robbie knew slightly from the Golf Club, and a woman called Jennifer Wilkinson, the Sales Director. As soon as he heard what she did he was more determined than ever that he didn't want the job. The boys at the Club wouldn't half give him stick about working for a woman.

Simpson gave his usual spiel about the long standing tradition of the family business as one of the largest building supplies companies in the country, how it had been started by his grandfather, continued on by his father and now developed into an international business by the present management, namely himself.

"And how could you see yourself contributing to the continuation of this tradition of success, Mr. Wilson?"

"Well, I believe very strongly that every generation has to do its bit if a family business is to keep on growing and succeeding. Too many sons and daughters forget that they have to work damned hard and not just spend the profits. It's great to see that the work ethic has survived to the present time in Simpson's; and that's what I can contribute - sheer hard work. In my book there's no substitute for honest graft."

It was clear to Robbie that his little speech was exactly what old Simpson wanted to hear. The Personnel guy wasn't really paying a lot of attention - probably thinking about how soon he could get away for a game of golf with his cronies. Jennifer Wilkinson was looking at him with frank disbelief, a faint smile puckering her lips. He realised she wasn't going to be taken in by any of that old baloney.

They took it in turns to quiz him. Simpson asked a few general questions before Personnel took over, running quickly through the details of his earlier career. Personnel liked to hear himself talk so Robbie was able to confine himself to a bland re-run of his time with O'Reilly's and then Mooney's.

He knew as soon as Jennifer Wilkinson started to question him that he was in trouble. She explored his previous experience in much more detail than Personnel and then, when the interview seemed to be coming to a close, she said

"Why did you bother to apply for this position, Mr Wilson? You seem to be well suited for it but you don't appear to be very interested in getting it."

Robbie reacted as if she had slapped him. He tried hard to mask his annoyance that she had so easily spotted the yawning gap between the quality of his application, which Caroline had insisted on vetting, and his interview performance.

"Miss Wilkinson," he started,

"Mrs, actually," she murmured.

"I'm sorry, Mrs Wilkinson," he began again, a sharp angry edge to his voice, "I applied for this job because I reckon I'm just about the best candidate you're likely to be able to find. If you had taken the time to look at my previous experience and the way I developed the business for both O'Reilly and Mooney you would have realised that before I came in here today. This company needs a good Sales Manager and I'm as good as they come. If you can't see that, too bad."

Simpson and Personnel looked at him open-mouthed and Jennifer Wilkinson, smiling, said quietly,

"'Thank you, Mr Wilson, I have no further questions."

"You'll hear from us in a few days, Mr Wilson." Personnel made no attempt to hide his contempt.

Robbie left the room, his mind in a whirl. He was angry with himself for letting Jennifer Wilkinson upset him so much. What did it matter after all? He didn't want the job and his outburst was likely to help on that score. So why be angry? He knew that she had been trying to wrong foot him and he'd fallen for it like a complete amateur. Working for her would be some crack; far too bloody clever by half!

The letter had come that morning. He made sure that he was closest to the front door when the postman slid the mail noisily through the letterbox. Fortunately, there were a couple of other letters as well, so he was able to slip the letter bearing the pretentious Simpson logo into his dressing gown pocket before anyone else saw it.

"Nothing much," he said, answering Caroline's unspoken question, "just the usual rubbish," as he lathered butter onto a slice of hot toast.

"Oh! I had such a feeling there would be something from Simpson's this morning."

Caroline's disappointment was plain. He sensed she'd already decided he was getting the job.

"It's been four days since the interviews. Surely it can't take them that long to make up their minds. There were only four people in for it and they couldn't seriously consider giving it to any of the other three. There's not one of them has your experience. They must have seen that. I nearly feel like ringing Jennie Wilkinson and asking her what's going on."

Robbie could hardly speak. The very idea that Caroline would consider ringing up that woman Wilkinson to find out if he had got the job took his breath away. Good God! Suppose they got talking about what had happened at the interview. He could hardly bear to think of what could happen.

"What do you mean ring her up?" he stammered at last. "How could you do that? I'd look a right bollocks if it got out that you had been ringing up to find out if I'd got the job or not. You'll do no such thing, do you hear?"

"All right, all right. No need to blow a gasket."

Caroline looked at him, the suspicion of a smile in her eyes.

"It's just that I was at school with Jennie so I know her well enough to call her. If you don't want me to, then I won't. But if we haven't heard anything by tomorrow you're going to have to ring to find out what's happening anyway. Must go or the kids will be late for school."

She knew Jennie Wilkinson! Caroline knew her! She wouldn't be long in letting Caroline know what a fool he had made of himself at the interview and how he'd lost the head. Christ, could he not even fix it so that he didn't get a job without the whole works falling on his head?

He sat looking at the letter, turning it over and over in his hands, wondering how he was going to explain the rejection to Caroline. He couldn't tell her that he had deliberately set out to blow the interview and that he had been downright rude to his potential boss. Caroline might be keen to push him as far as she could in his career but she was basically a very straightforward person, speaking her mind and not in any way devious. Or so he thought. How come she had never mentioned this Jennie Wilkinson before?

With an awful sense of foreboding he slipped his finger beneath the flap of the envelope and slowly, slowly prised it open.